Start Your Own

CHILD-CARE
SERVICE

Additional titles in *Entrepreneur's* **Startup Series**

Start Your Own

Bar and Tavern

Bed & Breakfast

Business on eBay

Business Support Service

Car Wash

Cleaning Service

Clothing Store

Coin-Operated Laundry

Consulting

Crafts Business

e-Business

e-Learning Business

Event Planning Business

Executive Recruiting Service

Florist Shop and Other Floral Businesses

Gift Basket Service

Growing and Selling Herbs and Herbal Products

Home Inspection Service

Import/Export Business

Information Consultant Business

Law Practice

Lawn Care Business

Mail Order Business

Medical Claims Billing Service

Personal Concierge Service

Personal Training Business

Pet-Sitting Business

Restaurant and Five Other Food Businesses

Self-Publishing Business

Seminar Production Business

Specialty Travel & Tour Business

Staffing Service

Successful Retail Business

Vending Business

Wedding Consultant Business

Wholesale Distribution Business

Entrepreneur
MAGAZINE'S

startup

Start Your Own

2ND EDITION

CHILD-CARE SERVICE

Your Step-by-Step
Guide to Success

Entrepreneur Press and Jacquelyn Lynn

Ep
Entrepreneur
Press

Editorial Director: Jere L. Calmes
Managing Editor: Marla Markman
Cover Design: Beth Hansen-Winter
Production: Eliot House Productions
Composition: Patricia Miller

This publication is designed to provide accurate and authoritative information in regard to the subject matter covered. It is sold with the understanding that the publisher is not engaged in rendering legal, accounting, or other professional services. If legal advice or other expert assistance is required, the services of a competent professional person should be sought.

Library of Congress Cataloging-in-Publication Data
Lynn, Jacquelyn.
    Start your own child-care service/by Entrepreneur Press and Jacquelyn Lynn.—2nd ed.
        p.   cm.
    Rev. ed. of: Child-care service / Jacquelyn Lynn. 2001.
    ISBN 1-59918-015-4 (alk. paper)
        1. Child care services—United States—Handbooks, manuals, etc. 2. Day care centers—United States—Handbooks, manuals, etc. 3. New business enterprises—United States—Handbooks, manuals, etc. I. Lynn, Jacquelyn. II. Lynn, Jacquelyn. Child-care service. III. Entrepreneur Press.

HQ778.63.S73 2006
362.71'202373—dc22   2006013265

Printed in Canada

12 11 10 09 08 07 06   10 9 8 7 6 5 4 3 2 1

Contents

Chapter 5

Chapter 6

Chapter 7

▲

Chapter 16

Preface

The number of working parents—including single-parent families and families with both parents employed—is climbing, creating an ever-growing need for quality child care. That need is creating a tremendous entrepreneurial opportunity for people who love children and want to build a business caring for them.

Child-care services range from small homebased operations to large commercial centers and can be started with an investment of as little as a few hundred dollars. You can stay very small, essentially just creating a job for yourself, or you can grow into a substantial enterprise with potentially millions of dollars a year in revenue.

You also have a tremendous amount of flexibility when it comes to the exact services you choose to offer. For example, you may limit your clientele to children in certain age groups or tailor your operating hours to meet the needs of a particular market segment. You may or may not want to provide transportation between your center and the children's homes and/or schools. You may want to take the children on field trips. As an alternative to child care, you may want to consider a business that focuses solely on providing transportation for children.

Of course, the basic work you will be doing—caring for someone else's children—bears a tremendous amount of responsibility and requires a serious commitment. When the children are in your custody, you are responsible for their safety and well-being. You will also play a key role in their overall development and may well be someone they'll remember their entire lives.

Regardless of the particular type of child-care service you want to start, this book will tell you how to do it. We'll start with an overview of the industry, look at the specific services you'll want to consider offering, and then go through the step-by-step process of setting up and running your new venture. You'll learn about basic requirements and start-up costs, day-to-day operations, and what to do when things don't go according to plan. We'll discuss how to find, hire, and keep good employees in an industry notorious for low pay and high turnover. You'll gain a solid understanding of the sales and marketing process, as well as how to track and manage the financial side of your business. Throughout the book, you will hear from child-care and child transportation business operators who have built successful companies and are eager to share what they learned in the process.

You will also need skills and knowledge to develop the content of a child-care program. This book is intended to provide both basic business information and specific design and operational material for the establishment and running of a child-care facility. You or your program director should have a background or familiarity with young children and their educational and developmental needs, and should look to other resources for program assistance.

Running a child-care center requires more than keeping the kids entertained. There must be a comprehensive philosophy and a concrete plan to implement it. Parents will expect your program to enrich their children as well as provide care. If you lack a strong background in educating children, consider taking college or community college courses in child development, education, and child psychology.

At various points in this book, scholastic terms such as "classroom" and "teacher" are used. A preschool license is different from a child-care center's license, and the curriculum concerns for a preschool are greater. However, child-care centers that stress an educational and enriching environment often adopt such terms to help parents understand that they are leaving their children in something more than a baby-sitting center. Child-care centers often divide children into groups by age and commonly refer to these groups as classes and the adults supervising them as teachers. This is neither inaccurate nor misleading if your child-care center is indeed geared toward fostering child development. However, we want to make it clear that this book discusses child-care centers, not preschools.

Whether you plan to start a small, family child-care center in your home or a large center at a commercial site, we recommend that you read every chapter in this book, because most of the information applies to all sizes and types of centers. We'd also like to suggest that you enjoy some peace and quiet now—as you read, study, and plan. Once your child-care center is up and running, your life will be full of the special noise and chaos—along with the intense satisfaction and rewards—that only happy children can create.

Introduction

One of the biggest challenges facing working American parents today is caring for their children. According to the Bureau of Labor Statistics, less than one-fourth of all families (about 22 percent) fit the traditional model of husband as wage-earner and wife as homemaker. In 61 percent of married-couple families, both husband and wife work outside the home. In more than half of married-couple families with children under age 6, both parents are employed. Nearly two-thirds of mothers with children under age 3 are working, and the labor-force participation of women in their childbearing years continues to expand. As the number of working parents in America rises, so will the demand for child care. In fact, according to the Urban Institute, more than 20 million children in the United States are regularly in nonparental care when they are not in school.

Smart Tip

Tip...

Take yourself and your business seriously. A child-care service is more than a glorified baby-sitter; it's a serious business providing an important service, and it's capable of generating a substantial income.

Another issue that has an impact on child-care issues is the new, 24-hour global market. Occupations with a high number of employees working nights and weekends—such as janitorial, hospitality, customer service, and technical support—are experiencing substantial growth, and workers in these fields are finding obtaining quality child care an even greater challenge than their 9-to-5 counterparts.

For many working parents, there is no single solution to their child-care needs. More than a third use more than one option, such as day-care centers part of the time and friends, neighbors, or relatives on other occasions. A recent study conducted by the Urban Institute, a nonprofit policy research organization, revealed that about 30 percent of working parents have two child-care arrangements, and another 8 percent are using at least three. The study found that 65 percent of the parents juggling multiple child-care arrangements use a combination of formal day-care centers, Head Start programs, and baby-sitting by relatives and friends. Another 20 percent use two separate day-care centers.

In addition to child care, parents also need transportation for their children. Kids who are too young to drive or take public transportation without supervision still need to get back and forth to school, as well as to places after school, whether it's to games, museums, libraries, music lessons, doctor's appointments, or whatever. But most parents can't leave their offices to take their children to these activities, so they're turning to transportation companies that specialize in schlepping children.

All this means opportunity for you. But before you take the leap into your own business, learn how others did it.

How Did They Start?

The successful child-care and child transportation service business owners interviewed for this book got their starts in a variety of ways.

A dare propelled Lois Mitten Rosenberry of Toledo, Ohio, into the child-care business. In 1982, through an internal political shake-up, she lost her job as the director of a church day-care center. She had two young children of her own, and if she got a job in a different field, she would need child care for her daughters. When she looked around at the child-care options available to her, she didn't like what she saw. And in the meantime, a number of parents of the children from the church center were asking her to open her own facility.

The idea was appealing, but, she felt, economically out of the question. Her husband got laid off shortly after she left the day-care center, and the only job he was able to find didn't pay enough to support the family, much less provide start-up capital for a new business. "Financially, we were absolutely at the end," she recalls. "My parents were making our house payment and giving us money for our living expenses, we qualified for the home energy assistance program, and our older daughter was on the free lunch program at school."

Mitten Rosenberry decided to ask her parents for a loan to open a child-care center. They agreed, but then she found out she was pregnant, and her parents withdrew their financial support for the business, saying her place was at home with her children. She argued, pointing out that running a child-care center was an excellent job for a working mother, but her parents were adamant. They would continue to help with living expenses, but they would not fund her business.

"I pretty much gave up on the idea," Mitten Rosenberry says. "Then I met with one of the parents who was anxious to get his daughter in our program and told him I couldn't get the funds. He said, 'I knew you wouldn't do it. I knew you'd get cold feet.' "

She took it as a dare, reacting at first with anger, then with determination. In 1982, she took out a second mortgage on the family home and was just one month away from the birth of her third child when she opened the first of seven Children's Discovery Centers in Toledo.

Janet Hale started caring for children in her home in Exeter, California, in 1980, when her own daughter was 2. She had been working as a bookkeeper but wanted to be at home with her child. She operated on her own for six years before forming a partnership with a friend who also had a family child-care center. Together, the two women leased a building that had housed a YMCA and opened their first commercial center in Exeter. Eventually, that partnership dissolved (amicably; the partner wanted to move to another state), but Hale continued to operate the commercial center and her own center at home. Soon Hale formed another partnership and bought a second commercial center in nearby Visalia. Three centers were more than Hale could handle, so she closed the one in her home to concentrate on the two commercial operations.

Suzanne Wright spent 18 years working full time for a biomedical research laboratory, but she cut back to part time when her daughter was born. A few months later, the company went out of business. Rather than look for another part-time position, she decided to start her own homebased child-care business in Ellicott City, Maryland, in 1991. Her second daughter was born two years later. "I continued providing child care

Stat Fact

According to the Bureau of Labor Statistics, in more than 18 million families with school-age children, one or both of the parents are employed. The gap between parents' work schedules and children's school schedules is typically 20 to 25 hours a week.

with the intention of returning to the 'outside' work force when my daughters entered elementary school," Wright says. "It is now 14 years later, and I am still in the child-care business."

Christine Srabian's story is similar. She wanted to stay home with her son, her sister was running a homebased child-care center, and she thought it was a great way to earn money and be at home. She started in 1992; though her son is a teenager, her child-care business near Baltimore continues to thrive.

Doris McNeill was a working mother when she saw the need for children's transportation in Gainesville, Florida, and saw an entrepreneurial opportunity for herself. When her daughter earned a place on a gymnastics team, McNeill's job prevented her from getting her daughter to practice. She says, "I thought there had to be other people who had the same problem, so Kids on Wheels was born."

Who's Running the Centers?

What are the characteristics of a person who would do well operating a child-care center? Mitten Rosenberry answers, "The person needs to be energetic, business-minded, a competent leader, have a pleasant personality, be professional, be willing to take calculated risks, be a good role model, have strong financial resources, be consistent in expectations of the staff, and be consistent in the delivery of service."

If you're going to be running a family child-care center, you should enjoy children. Hale says, "A person who is going to own a child-care center needs to love children, be a people person, have a high tolerance for stress, have good insurance, and have some management skills."

A child-care business can easily be started in your home with just a few weeks of planning and a modest amount of start-up cash. A commercially located center takes a greater investment of time, energy, and money. The size and type of business you choose will depend on your start-up resources and goals for the future. Many child-care providers are satisfied with a one-person operation in their home that generates a comfortable income while allowing them to do work they enjoy (and possibly even care for their own children). Others may start at home and eventually move to a commercial site as the business grows. Still others begin in a commercial location and are either content with one site or have plans to expand.

A special note if you're planning to care for children in your home: Homebased child-care centers are known as family child-care businesses, and they have changed significantly in recent years. As recently as 25 years ago, most providers charged by the hour, and they didn't get paid if a child didn't show at the last minute. Fees were the same for children of all ages, and there were few written contracts and no paid holidays or vacations. Even the providers didn't view their work as a professional service.

Today, family child-care providers are increasingly likely to see their work as a business. They love children and enjoy what they do, but they are taking a more professional approach to how they manage their operations. By reading this book before you open your business, you will be starting off on the right foot, and you won't face resistance down the road if you try to upgrade your operation and implement new procedures.

Who Is Your Market?

Prime candidates who need full-time child care are parents with infants to five-year-olds. Parents with children over five are good prospects for after-school care programs. The market segments most likely to use child-care services are dual-income families and single-parent households in most income brackets. A number of government programs help low-income families pay for child care so the adults can stay in the work force.

Within this very broad market is the more narrow group of clients you will serve. Use market research to figure out who these people are and how you can best attract them to your center. Mitten Rosenberry says the primary market at five of her seven locations is parents who are upper-income working professionals; the other two centers serve a number of middle-income families as well as those being subsidized by public funds. Hale says about half her clientele consists of dual-income families, and the other half is single mothers who receive government assistance as they work through programs designed to get them off welfare.

The goal of market research is to identify your market, find out where it is, and develop a strategy to communicate with prospective customers in a way that will convince them to bring their children to you.

When Mitten Rosenberry opened her first center, her demographic research revealed that there were 9,000 children from infant to five years old within a five-mile radius of the site; half the preschool children in the area were in day care of some sort because their mothers (or both parents) worked; and the number of households in the area was expected to double

Stat Fact

According to the Urban Institute, for more than half of pre-school children with employed mothers, the primary child-care provider is not related to the child; 32 percent of these children are in center-based child-care arrangements; and 16 percent are in family child-care centers. About 6 percent are cared for by a baby-sitter or nanny in the child's home.

within a decade. Contained in that five-mile radius were six child-care centers serving approximately 800 children.

Srabian's research was not as sophisticated. She lives in a very large planned community (about 5,000 homes), and the evidence of children needing care was obvious to her. That, and wanting to stay home with her son, prompted her to start her child-care business. Because children's transportation is a relatively new business segment, many providers are the first in their communities. Study the demographics of the area (available through the Census Bureau) to determine if the market will support your operation. How many children are under the age of 18? How many workers are commuting a half-hour, hour or more (which means they may not be able to drive their children to school and other activities)? What is the income range of families with children? You need to be sure you'll have customers and that they can afford your services. Next, study the competition. Call the local public transportation service and see what they offer. Call private schools to see if they have their own transportation and whether or not they use (or will refer to) private companies.

Before 9 and After 5

A growing market segment for child-care providers is parents who work nontraditional hours, including evenings, nights, and weekends. There are no statistics on the number of child-care centers that operate in the evenings and on the weekends, but experts say supply doesn't meet demand.

There have been documented cases of workers at round-the-clock manufacturing facilities using their cars as "child care" of last resort. At one food processing plant in western Idaho, young children were put to sleep and left unattended in cars in the plant's parking lot.

The issue of child care during nonstandard hours is growing in importance due to a number of major trends. The long-term trend toward a service-based economy has led to the operation of more businesses during early mornings, evenings, nights, and weekends. Employers in all sectors are changing their schedules for reasons ranging from increased flexibility to enhanced customer satisfaction to reduced air pollution. A significant percentage of employees working nonstandard hours are women and mothers. Neighbors and grandmothers, the traditional sources of informal child care when the parents are not available, are also less likely to be found at home. They, too, are increasingly in the labor force.

Does this mean you should open a 24-hour child-care facility? Not necessarily. Though the demand is certainly there, many parents needing

Bright Idea
Maximize your investment in facilities by offering child-care services during nontraditional hours, such as evenings, nights, and weekends.

such a service earn low to moderate incomes and cannot afford to pay a lot for child care. Providers also find that extended hours cut into their own personal time and that it is difficult to recruit and retain staff for nonstandard hours. But if you can figure out a way to overcome the obstacles, offering care during nontraditional hours can provide a valuable service while allowing you to maximize your facility.

First Things First

Many start-up businesses are challenged by a lack of information and resources, but that is not the case for child-care providers. You have a wealth of public and private resources to turn to for advice, support, training, and even funding.

Most communities have child-care resource and referral agencies (R&Rs) that can help you with a variety of issues, such as licensing, setting rates, and even lending you toys and equipment. Once you're in business, these agencies will also refer families to you for your services. Make finding that agency your first priority after you finish this book. If you are not familiar with the agency nearest you, check with the National Child Care Information Center or the National Association for Family Child Care for assistance (see Appendix).

Your next step is to identify the various government agencies that oversee child-care providers. A good place to start is with your state's information department (look in the government section of your telephone directory). In most cases, you will find yourself dealing with multiple agencies with different and sometimes overlapping responsibilities. These agencies will tell you what is required to get your doors open for business. Consolidate their information and create your own start-up checklist like the one on page 8.

Buying an Existing Child-Care Service

Owning a child-care center doesn't necessarily require building the company from scratch. You might want to consider buying an existing child-care center, which is how Janet Hale acquired her second commercial center. If the appeal of being in business for yourself is in running the company rather than starting it, this route to business ownership is an option worth investigating. It allows you to bypass all the steps involved in creating a business infrastructure because the original owner has already done that. You can take over an operation that is already generating cash flow—and perhaps even profits. You will have a history on which to build your forecasts and a future that includes an established customer base. And there's generally less risk involved in buying an existing concern than there is in creating a whole new company.

Of course, there are drawbacks to buying a business. Though the actual dollar amounts depend on the size and type of business, it often takes more cash to buy an existing business than to start one yourself. When you buy a company's assets, you usually get stuck with at least some of its liabilities. And it's highly unlikely that you'll find an existing business that is precisely the company you would have built on your own. Even so, you just might find that the business you want is currently owned by someone else.

Why do people sell businesses—especially profitable ones? For a variety of reasons. Many entrepreneurs are happiest during the start-up and early growth stages of a company; once the business is running smoothly, they get bored and begin looking for something new. Other business owners may grow tired of the responsibility or face

Start-Up Checklist

Use this checklist (and tailor it to your own needs) to make sure you've covered all your bases before starting your business.

❑ *Type of center.* Will you operate from your home or a commercial location?

❑ *Licensing.* What licenses are you required to have and from which agencies? What are the requirements, costs, and lead times?

❑ *Training and certification.* What type of training and/or certification do you need?

❑ *Market.* What are the child-care needs of your community?

❑ *Location.* Choose a site that is appropriate and affordable.

❑ *Legal requirements.* Check on zoning and any other legal issues.

❑ *Financial issues.* Estimate your start-up costs and identify the source(s) of your start-up funds.

❑ *Health and safety issues.* Plan for accident and illness prevention, and develop emergency procedures.

❑ *Programs.* Develop an appropriate schedule of activities for the children.

❑ *Equipment.* What do you need to adequately equip your center, where will you get it, and how much will it cost?

❑ *Insurance.* What coverage do you need to adequately protect yourself and the children in your care?

❑ *Staffing.* If you plan to hire people, know the required staff-to-child ratios and develop your human resources policies.

❑ *Links.* What community and professional resources are available to you?

health or other personal issues that motivate them to sell their companies. Some of the most successful entrepreneurs go into business with a solid plan for how they're going to get out of the business when the time comes.

If you decide to shop around for an existing child-care center, look at every service provider in the area that meets your requirements. Just because it isn't on the market doesn't mean it isn't for sale. Use your networking skills to find potential companies; let friends and professional colleagues know what you're looking for. You might even consider placing a "wanted to buy" classified ad.

Smart Tip *Tip...*

If you buy an existing child-care center, include a noncompete clause in your terms of sale. Your new business won't be worth much if the seller opens a competing operation down the street a few weeks after you take over the old company.

Evaluating a Company

One of the most challenging financial calculations is figuring out what a business is worth. Research the selling price and terms of recently sold child-care centers in your area, and use them as a guide. You may value the company based on its after-tax cash flow or on the value of the company's assets, if they were liquidated, minus its debts and liabilities. You should call on your financial advisors to assist you with these calculations.

The figures are only part of the equation. Elements that are not as easy to assign a value to include the center's reputation and the strength of the relationship the current owner has with parents, suppliers, and employees.

Thorough due diligence is an essential part of the acquisition process. This includes reviewing, auditing, and verifying all relevant information regarding the business, so you'll know exactly what you are buying and from whom. Have your accountant assist you in evaluating the financial statements, your banker help with financing issues, and your attorney guide you in researching the legal aspects of buying the business. And remember that you can walk away from the deal at any point in the negotiation process before a contract is signed.

Outlook for the Future

Child-care center operators agree the future is bright. The need for services will continue to increase, and the options and opportunities should also expand.

Mitten Rosenberry is seeing an increase in the number of corporations that contact her looking for a center to meet the needs of their employees. While they don't want to subsidize a center as they may have done in the past, they are willing to make some concessions, such as with the land or building, to get a center in operation near their offices. "There will be more opportunities to move into some business parks, but the enticements will probably not be as big as they were at one time," she says.

Of course, there will always be challenges. Labor will continue to be tight, and this is definitely a labor-intensive business. Depending on individual market conditions, very small operators may find it tough to compete with larger chains for both employees and customers. And if you build a solid, profitable commercial center, you may find yourself the target of takeover attempts. "I've been approached by several companies that wanted to buy me out," Mitten Rosenberry says. "They figure if they can buy a successful operation, that allows them to immediately pick up another 10 percent in volume and keep on growing."

Beware!

Do enough research before opening your child-care service so you meet all your state's legal requirements and are able to operate a quality center. However, don't get so bogged down in the research process that you don't get your business open. You'll never know everything, and if you wait until you do, you'll never get started.

Services
and Policies

Before you open your doors to the first child, you should decide on the services you will provide and the policies that will guide your operation. To simply say you are going to "take care of children" is woefully inadequate. How many children? What ages? What hours? Will you provide food or ask their parents to? What activities will you offer? What sort of price and payment policies will you have? And the list goes on.

A comprehensive business plan is essential to a smooth-running, successful, and profitable child-care business. Chapter 4 of this book will tell you more about putting together your business plan and integrating the various parts, but the foundation of any child-care operation is its services and policies.

Your first step is to check with the appropriate regulatory agencies to find out what's involved in providing particular services. For example, each state has its own guidelines for the maximum number of children and maximum number in each age group in a family child-care facility. States also have guidelines regarding the number of caregivers required per number of children in each age group for commercial facilities. There will likely be other requirements and restrictions, depending on the type of facility you run.

Services

Decide what services to offer based on your own preferences and what your market research says your community needs. Your choices include:

- Full-time care during traditional weekday hours
- After-school care
- Nontraditional hours (very early mornings, evenings, overnight care, weekdays, and/or weekends)
- Drop-in or on-demand care, either during traditional or nontraditional hours
- Part-time care
- Parents' night out (weekend evening care)
- Age-based care
- Transportation

Lois Mitten Rosenberry's centers (Children's Discovery Center and Discover Express) in Toledo, Ohio, offer full-day child care, generally from 6:30 A.M. to 6 P.M., serving children from six weeks old through kindergarten age. She also has a before- and after-school program for school-age children, as well as a preschool program. Transportation services are limited to occasional field trips and shuttling children between the centers for special programs as necessary.

Suzanne Wright's hours are Monday through Thursday, 7:30 A.M. to 5 P.M., and she provides care for infants and children up to four years old. Christine Srabian's hours are from 7 A.M. to 5:30 P.M. Monday through Friday. She has youngsters for full days, some before and after school, and some who come just a few days a week.

Kids on Wheels, Doris McNeill's children's transportation service, takes kids to and from school and child-care providers, as well as to and from after-school activities and other events—even to doctor's appointments when the parents are unable to do it themselves.

Consider offering a "mother's day out" program to give stay-at-home moms a safe place to leave their youngsters for a few hours each week. Generally, such programs will have greater utilization in more affluent areas. Your program may include three hours in the morning or afternoon two or three days a week. Children in a half-day program do not need lunch, but you may want to feed them a snack. If you offer after-school care, you can balance your workload by offering a "mother's day out" program in the morning. You might also want to occasionally offer a parents' night out once in a while, so that the parents of the youngsters you care for can have an evening out knowing their children are in a familiar, safe place with a caregiver they know and trust.

> **Bright Idea**
>
> Don't try to do it all at once; keep your service menu simple in the beginning. As you gain experience and confidence, you can add additional services that will expand your business and increase your revenue.

Policies

It's important that you think through your policies completely before you open for business. Give each parent a copy of your policies as part of their contract, and have them sign an acknowledgment that they've read, understand, and agree to abide by your rules. There is less chance for misunderstanding if the information is clearly stated and agreed to by parents. Your policies and contract do not have to be written in formal, legal language; in fact, it's better if they are written in everyday terms that are easily understood.

As you develop and communicate your policies, remember that you are a professional and deserve to be treated with respect and consideration.

Confidentiality and Access to Records

Establish policies and procedures covering the exchange of information among parents, your staff, and other professionals or agencies that are involved with the child and family before the child enters your care, during the time you are caring for the child, and after the child leaves.

The child's record should be available to the parents for inspection at all times. The exchange of information about the child and family among various service providers can greatly enhance the effectiveness of child and family support; however, it should be accomplished with sensitivity to issues of confidentiality and the need to know. The responsibility for a child's health and well-being is shared by all those involved in the child's care: parents, health professionals, and caregivers. You should expect parents to

Information, Please

Caring for a child adequately means you need to have a certain amount of personal information about that child and his or her family. When you need to ask for personal information, begin by explaining to the parent why you need it and how you're going to use it.

For example, you may need to know something about the parents' religious beliefs to respond appropriately to a question or comment the child makes during the day. Or a child may be worried about something that is going on at home; if you have an understanding of the situation, you'll be in a better position to help the child deal with his or her feelings and fears.

provide you with all necessary and appropriate health information; typically, this will be accomplished by the parents completing certain forms, but it may also require telephone or face-to-face conversations for clarification or additional information. You and your staff should not disclose any material in a child's record to anyone without the written consent of the parents or legal guardian. Even among your staff, confidential information should be seen by and only discussed with staff who need the information to provide services.

Fees

Deciding how much to charge is discussed in Chapter 5. In terms of policies, however, what's important when it comes to fees is consistency. It's not good business practice to charge one person less or to provide free services to someone else—and if you do, chances are the parents will find out and be upset.

Some fee policies you'll want to consider include:

- If a family has more than one child in your center, you might discount the rate for the second child.
- You may want to set fees based on age, because younger children require more attention. Along these lines, you may also consider whether or not a child is toilet-trained when deciding what to charge.
- Even the most conscientious parents will occasionally be late picking up their child. How will you charge parents for the extra work this causes you?

Hours of Operation

Your hours of operation will be dictated by the type of service you provide, but they should be clearly stated to avoid any misunderstanding.

As part of this policy, you might also indicate what circumstances would cause a special closing. For example, you might consider a policy stating that you will be closed on any day(s) the local public school system closes for an emergency or natural disaster situation.

Holidays

Stipulate the holidays you will close for and whether or not you expect to be paid for those days. For example, Wright's contract includes 12 fully paid holidays.

Vacations

If parents expect you to reserve a space in your program during the child's absence (whether due to vacation or extended illness), they should be required to continue paying for it.

How you handle this depends on the demand for space in your center and the size and nature of your competition. A common arrangement is to discount the regular tuition up to 50 percent for any full week the child misses. Mitten Rosenberry charges half price for the time the child is absent, up to four weeks. "Four weeks is the most we will hold a place, because our expenses go on just the same," she says. Many providers, including Srabian and Wright, charge the full fee whether the child attends or not.

As part of your vacation policy, you may want to specify how much advance notice you require when children are going to be taken out of your center for vacations. Such advance notice may allow you to temporarily fill the gap with another child so you can still earn full pay on those days.

Speaking of vacations, what about your own? If you are operating a commercial center or a large, family child-care program, you may have sufficient staff so you can take off for a week without any disruption in service. But if you run a small, family day-care center, taking a vacation may require you to shut down your operation.

Vacations are important, and you need time away from your business to rest, relax, and spend quality time with your own family. Decide how much time off you're going to take, whether you're going to shut down or find someone to take over for you, and whether or not you will require parents to pay for the time you are closed. For example, Wright takes 10 days of vacation a year, and her clients pay half of their regular rate while she's off. However you handle your vacations, make sure it's all spelled out in the policy statement you give parents.

Bright Idea

Plan your time off well in advance, especially if you run a family child-care center. Post a schedule at the beginning of the year, letting your customers know when you will be closed for vacation and/or long weekends.

Absences

Parents are contracting with you to care for their children during a certain period of time, and your general policy should provide that you be paid for this time whether the child is actually in your facility or not. You may make an exception for planned vacations when you have ample notice (as previously discussed), but in most cases, you should not be expected to sacrifice your income when a child is absent for one or two days during the week, regardless of the reason. After all, most of your expenses will continue whether the child is there or not.

Transportation

Usually, transportation of children between the center and home is the responsibility of the parent or the guardian. Transportation between the center and school is often provided by centers that offer after-school care—vital to many working parents who are unable to pick their children up after school. You may provide transportation on a limited basis for youngsters participating in field trips. For more on offering transportation, either as an adjunct to your child-care service or as an independent business, see Chapter 10.

Chronic Misbehavior and Other Adjustment Issues

Young children all have off days, and even the sweetest child can be an intolerable monster on occasion. Providing care for children requires considerable patience and understanding. However, a child who is a continual disruptive influence should not be tolerated, particularly if the misbehavior involves harm or the risk of harm to other children.

You need an expulsion policy to allow you to remove disruptive children from your care. Three warnings or reports of misbehavior should be sufficient to allow the parent to instruct the child to behave properly. After that, you may inform the parents that they will have to find child care elsewhere. While you may want to work with the child to help correct a behavior problem, you cannot allow one youngster to directly harm his or her playmates, or to create such a drain on staff time and resources that your other charges are neglected. Spell this out in your policy.

Mitten Rosenberry's policy on this subject reads: "If a child is unable to adjust to our program, is consistently insubordinate, or has a serious behavioral problem, we reserve the right to suspend or terminate his or her enrollment."

Bright Idea

To be sure parents stay current on any changes in your policies, ask them to sign a new contract periodically, perhaps every six months or at least once a year. The contract should include a copy of your current policies and guidelines, and point out any changes, whether or not those changes affect every child.

Care of Sick Children

Generally, most child-care centers do not care for sick children and have policies stating that if a child becomes ill while at the center, he or she must be picked up within a certain amount of time. Some hospitals provide outpatient day care for youngsters too sick to be in school or a child-care center but not sick enough to require hospitalization; check around in your community to see what services are available so you can make referrals if necessary.

You will encounter situations when a child is not sick in terms of having a contagious condition or needing any special care, but he or she requires medication. You need to decide if you will administer medication and what you require from the parents if you do. See "Administering Medication" on page 22.

Sick Days

Infections spread quickly among children, so if you notice any symptom of illness, you should immediately separate the child from the other youngsters and contact the parents to have the child picked up. If the child does not respond to you, is having trouble breathing, or is having a convulsion, call 911.

The symptoms that necessitate removing a child from the child-care setting include:

- ○ Fever and sore throat, rash, vomiting, diarrhea, earache, irritability, or confusion. Fever is defined as having a temperature of 100 degrees taken orally or 102 degrees taken rectally. For children 4 months old or younger, the lower rectal temperature of 101 degrees is considered a fever threshold.
- ○ Diarrhea (runny, watery, or bloody stools)
- ○ Vomiting two or more times in a 24-hour period
- ○ Body rash with fever
- ○ Sore throat with fever and swollen glands
- ○ Severe coughing (child gets red or blue in the face or makes a high-pitched whooping sound after coughing)
- ○ Eye discharge (thick mucous or pus draining from the eye, or pinkeye)
- ○ Yellowish skin or eyes
- ○ Irritability, continuous crying, or anything requiring more attention than you can provide without jeopardizing the health and safety of other children in your care

Late Pickup

You should set policies regarding the consequences of failing to pick children up as scheduled. You may charge a fee to compensate you or your staff for the resulting overtime, and that fee might escalate if the parent is habitually late. Chronic late pickups may be sufficient cause to terminate your arrangement. If you feel this way, make it clear in your policy.

If you are a family child-care provider, you may find it necessary to create a similar policy for parents who drop their children off early.

At Gingerbread House, Janet Hale's policy includes the provision that when a parent is late, she attempts to call the parents, then starts calling the people on the emergency pickup list in the child's file. The late fee—$5 for the first 10 minutes and $1 per minute thereafter—must be paid the next day. "We charge a steep fee because our teachers have lives," she says. "But if we can't find anybody to pick up the child, we stay here until someone comes."

Srabian's policy calls for a payment of $5 for every 15 minutes the parent is late, but she doesn't always charge it. For example, she understands that parents can get stuck in traffic, so she doesn't charge under those circumstances. But if the parent has control over the situation and chooses to be late, the charge applies.

> **Tip...**
>
> **Smart Tip**
>
> Your policy statement should encourage parents to have a backup source of child care in case you are unavailable (if you are ill or on vacation) or your center is inaccessible (perhaps due to some sort of physical damage like a flood or fire) for any reason.

Meals

Your program can include complete menu planning and food preparation or require parents to send meals and snacks along with their children each day. A compromise would be to have children bring their own lunches while you provide drinks and snacks. You might also want to consider offering breakfast and/or dinner, depending on your operating hours and the needs of the parents. Your meal policy should include any special information about feeding infants. Chapter 8 discusses equipping your kitchen and food storage and preparation issues.

> **Tip...**
>
> **Smart Tip**
>
> Maintain records of the recipes you use when preparing food for the children for at least one year (longer if required by law).

You should develop a written policy about food brought from home. It should meet the child's nutritional requirements and should be clearly labeled with the child's name, the date, and the type of food. The food should be stored at an appropriate temperature until eaten. Food brought from one child's home should never be fed to another child, and children should not be allowed to share their food.

Smart Tip

Review your contract and policies at least once a year to make sure they are still accurate and appropriate for your operation. If you make changes, provide each parent with a copy of the new information, and have them sign a statement saying they have read, understand, and agree to abide by the policy and/or contract changes.

Emergencies

For each child, you should have emergency contact information on file and an emergency consent form that would allow you to take that child to a doctor or hospital in the event of an accident, illness, or any other situation that may require immediate medical attention.

Health Issues

Parents should provide written proof that children are current on their vaccinations. Also, you need to know the details of any health or medical conditions (such as allergies, asthma, diabetes, epilepsy, and sickle cell anemia) that may require immediate action. You should know what happens to the child during a crisis related to the condition, how to prevent such a crisis, how to deal with the crisis, and whether you need training in a particular emergency procedure.

Smoking, Alcohol, and Drugs

Have a written policy stating that smoking tobacco (cigars, cigarettes, or pipes) and using or having illegal drugs is prohibited in your facility at all times, and that alcohol use is prohibited when children are in your care.

No children should be exposed to cigarette smoke. Inhaling secondhand cigarette smoke has been linked to respiratory problems in children. Children exposed to smoke are at increased risk of developing bronchitis, pneumonia, and otitis media (infection of the middle ear behind the eardrum) when they get common respiratory infections such as colds. Children with asthma are especially in danger of having their condition worsen when they are exposed to cigarette smoke. Smoking in rooms other than those the children occupy is not a sufficient remedy. Smoke gets into the ventilation system and is distributed throughout the building. Therefore, no smoking should be allowed at any time in any home or building that children occupy.

Release of Children

To ensure the safety and security of the children in your care, you should maintain a log for parents to sign children in and out of your facility. Parents should note the date, time, child's name, and name of the person dropping off or picking up the child.

You should also maintain a file of the names, addresses, and telephone numbers of persons authorized to pick up each child in your care. You should only release a child to a person for whom you have written consent by the custodial parent. Never honor a telephone authorization unless there is prior written consent by the custodial parent on file. Telephone authorization could be falsely provided by a person pretending to be the child's custodial parent.

Contact your local police department for advice on how to avoid releasing a child into an unsafe situation, such as to a parent who appears to be intoxicated (under the influence of drugs or alcohol). Have a written policy and inform all parents/guardians of it when the child is admitted to your care.

> **Bright Idea**
>
> Require each child to bring a clean change of clothes every day so they have something to wear if they become wet or soiled.

Other Policies

Your policy statement or center handbook should cover everything a parent needs to know about how you operate. Some points to consider include:

- Your general philosophy about children and what they need.
- Minimum and maximum ages for children in your care.
- What types of activities you offer.
- Restricting what children may bring with them because it's difficult to keep track of toys from home.
- If you handle toilet training, and how.
- What you expect of parents.

Admission Procedures

The first step in the admission process is to give the parents and child a guided tour of your facility. This gives you (or your director) an opportunity to sell the advantages of structured play with other youngsters over simple baby-sitting. As you demonstrate the quality of your center, the exposure to the equipment, play areas, and other children will probably excite the child.

You'll need to find out what days and hours the parents need services, and if you have a space available for the child. You might also inquire about previous child-care arrangements and find out why the parents are seeking care. At the conclusion of the tour, provide the parents with printed materials, such as a brochure on the center and your policies.

If you are a family child-care center, an in-person interview with the parents and child is especially important because the child will be spending a substantial portion of his or her waking hours in your home. If for any reason you feel like it won't work out, be honest—but tactful—and tell the parents. After all, it's your home and your business, and you have a right to decide who you'll care for. You may want to accept children on a trial basis of two to four weeks, with the understanding that both you and the parents have the right to terminate your services for any reason.

A written contract outlining the services you are providing, the fee amount and payment terms, and your policies should be completed and signed by both you and the parents before the child's first day. You should also insist that all enrollment forms be completed before the child is admitted.

Safety Standards and Policies

The issue of safety is an integral part of everything you do in the operation of your child-care center, and safety-related issues are mentioned throughout this book. This section will include issues and concerns not discussed elsewhere.

- *Inspections.* All licensed child-care centers are subject to occasional inspection. When any deficiencies are identified during an inspection or review by a licensing agency, funding agency, accreditation organization, or other regulatory department, you should develop a written plan for the resolution. The plan should include a description of the problem, proposed timeline for the resolution, designation of responsibility for correcting the deficiency, and a description of the successful resolution of the problem.

  Simple problems that can be immediately corrected do not require extensive documentation. For these, a brief notation that the problem was identified and corrected is sufficient. But documentation is still necessary, so that recurring problems can be addressed by a more lasting solution.

- *Fire safety.* Fire extinguishers should be inspected every three months, and a record of such inspections and any maintenance kept on file. Regular evacuation drills should be held and records of such events kept on file.

- *Food and nutrition.* You should maintain records covering your nutrition services budget, expenditures for food, numbers and types of meals served daily, and inspection reports made by health authorities. Retain this information for at least one year or the length of time required by your state.

- *Health department reporting requirements.* Certain diseases or conditions among your staff or the children in your care must be reported to the local health department. Contact your local health department for complete information on reporting requirements and procedures.

Children with Special Needs

The Americans with Disabilities Act requires that reasonable accommodation should be given to people with disabilities. The law covers children with disabilities seeking reasonable accommodation in a child-care setting. In addition to making physical changes, such as installing ramps, wide doors, and restrooms that can accommodate children in wheelchairs, you may need to provide for a child's special physical, emotional, or psychological needs. Other special needs may include assistance with feeding, following special dietary requirements, giving medicines and/or performing medical procedures, and ensuring that special equipment operates or is used properly.

Be sure you can comfortably answer the following questions:

- Does the child's disability require more care than you are reasonably able to provide?
- Do you have the skills and abilities needed to perform medical or other duties required for the child's care, or can you readily obtain those skills?
- Is your facility equipped to meet the health and safety needs of this child?
- Is the extra time you will need to devote to caring for this child more than you can handle without putting the other children at increased risk for illness or injury, or without causing you to neglect their needs?

In deciding whether to admit a child with special needs, you should meet with the child's parents and health-care providers to discuss the particular needs of the child. In most cases, the accommodations required by the Americans with Disabilities Act are compatible with a safe and healthy environment in which all the children in the child-care facility can thrive. As a provider responsible for all the children in your care, you should ensure that the extra demands on your time to care for a child with special needs is supported by additional resources, including help from experts, as needed. You should work with the child's parents and health-care professionals to make sure you have the support you need.

Administering Medication

Some children in your child-care facility may need to take medication during the hours you care for them. Before agreeing to give any medication, whether prescription or over-the-counter, obtain written permission from the parent. Also, check with your local child-care licensing agency regarding local regulations on administering medication.

You should make sure that any prescribed medication you give to a child:

- has the first and last name of the child on the container.
- has been prescribed by a licensed health professional. Check to see that the name and phone number of the health professional who ordered the medication is on the container.
- is in the original package or container.
- has the date the prescription was filled.

- has an expiration date.
- has specific instructions for giving, storing, and disposing of the medication.
- is in a childproof container.

You may want to suggest that parents ask their pharmacist to divide the medications into two separate bottles, one to be kept at home and one to be kept at the child-care facility. This way, children will be less likely to miss a dose of their prescription due to parents forgetting to bring medications to the facility or to take them home at night.

A parent may ask that you give a child an over-the-counter medication, such as acetaminophen (Tylenol and other brand names). Such medications should be treated with the same respect and care as prescription drugs. Over-the-counter medication for each child should be labeled with:

- The child's first and last names
- The current date
- The expiration date
- Specific instructions for giving, storing, and disposing of the medication
- The name of the health-care provider who recommended the medication

If the child is under two years of age, check your state licensing regulations. Some states do not allow a provider to administer over-the-counter medications to children under two years of age.

If a child is mistakenly given another child's medication, call the poison control center immediately and follow the advice given. Then call the physician and parents of the child who mistakenly received the medication. All medications should have childproof caps and be stored out of reach of children. Medications requiring refrigeration should be clearly marked and separated from food. You may want to keep all medications in a separate, covered container marked "Medications" within the refrigerator.

Never use medications after the expiration date. Also, do not allow parents to add medications to bottles of formula or milk brought from home. This can lead to inadvertent overdoses.

You should keep a medication record in your child-care facility. The record should list:

- The child's name
- The name of the medication and how and when it is to be given
- The parent's signature of consent

You should also keep a log documenting when you give medications. Each time you give a child a medication, you should list the date, time, child's name, name of the medication, and dosage given. If more than one provider in your facility administers medication, the provider who gave the child the medicine should initial the entry. Your medication log might look like the one on page 24.

Medication Log

Date	Time	Child's Name	Name of Medication	Dose Given	Initials

Running Your
Child-Care
Business

Caring for children can be enjoyable and rewarding, but if you are taking care of other people's children and accepting compensation for it, then caring for children is a business, and it needs to be managed accordingly. Even though you probably want to get into this business because you love children and not because you love to keep records, pay taxes, and worry about staffing, you must do these tasks effectively if you're going to maintain a viable operation.

The high rate of attrition in the child-care business is driven in large part by the fact that many caregivers focus almost entirely on nurturing and caring for the children in their charge, and neglect the financial and management sides of their operation. But whether your goal is to run a small, family child-care center or to build a chain of commercial locations, you must deal with administration and management issues if your business is going to survive. If you plan ahead, that won't be hard.

Set up your financial record-keeping system from the outset in a way that will provide you with the information you need to monitor your profitability and handle your

Principle Over Profit

By the time Lois Mitten Rosenberry had three thriving centers in the Toledo, Ohio, area, she decided to expand to Columbus. She put together plans for a state-of-the-art center, and city representatives welcomed her enthusiastically. Then she applied for an SBA loan, and it was approved—but on terms she couldn't accept.

Because of her strong Christian faith, part of the curriculum at each of her centers involves reading and discussing a Bible story once a week. The Bible stories are used to teach lessons in basic values, and teachers are careful not to prejudice the children against the faith of their parents.

"We figured that less than 1 percent of the time the children are with us had anything to do with anything religious at all," Mitten Rosenberry says. "We are not a church; we are a high-quality child-care center." Even so, she was committed to maintaining a degree of spiritual education, using Biblical tales to teach contemporary values.

But the SBA stipulated that she could have the funds for the Columbus center only on the condition that she never mention God to the children. "I knew right then that if I said 'OK, I want this million-dollar center at any price,' it would be empty success for me." She refused the loan and appealed the restriction, ultimately filing a lawsuit against the federal government in 1992. The case began winding its way through the courts with decisions going first one way and then the other. "It went to the Sixth District Circuit Court of Appeals—one step away from the Supreme Court—but we won," she says.

It is one of life's ironies that while the lawsuit was pending, Mitten Rosenberry was honored as the 1993 Small-Business Person of the Year for the Toledo and Cleveland District of the SBA. And though she ultimately won the suit, during the appeals process she lost the Columbus site and $30,000 in early development costs.

tax reporting. You may want to hire a consultant or an accountant who specializes in small businesses to help you at first; this small investment could save you a substantial amount of time and money in the long run. For more about financial management, see Chapter 5. Commit yourself to monitoring your profitability on at least a monthly basis.

Expect to spend a significant amount of time on management, marketing, and administration. If you have employees, they need to be trained and supervised. Though the demand for child care is high, parents won't be able to find you if you don't market your service. And keeping up with administrative details—paying bills, buying supplies, doing budgets and forecasts, meeting ongoing licensing requirements, facility maintenance, etc.—is a never-ending process.

If your goal is a sizable commercial center, you're not likely to spend much time actually caring for children. Lois Mitten Rosenberry spends plenty of time in her seven centers around the children, she hasn't actually been a caregiver for at least 15 years.

"I made a very conscious decision when I began," she explains. "I knew I could hire a secretary to cover the office and I could be a teacher in the classroom. Or I could be the one in the office, and I could hire the teacher. I decided it was better for me to be the one in the office answering the phone and giving the tours because no one else had as much invested in this business as I did. A secretary might go through the motions and give out information, but a secretary is not going to convey the same passion that I'm going to convey when I know I'm responsible for meeting payroll on Friday night." In the beginning, you may double as a caregiver as well as the director, but, Mitten Rosenberry adds, "You don't want to get in the habit of doing that on a regular basis, or your program will suffer." Her seven centers employ more than 165 people.

Children's Records

The record-keeping requirements of a child-care service are greater than those of most small businesses. The financial side (tracking income and expenses) is fairly basic, but you need to maintain a substantial amount of information on each child in your care. Some of this information is required by law, and some you will obtain to improve your service and strengthen your relationship with the children and their parents.

Set up a file for each child in your care. It should include a comprehensive information form (see the sample on page 29), any necessary special consent forms (such as for travel or administering medication), medical information, attendance records, incident reports, and any other notes or observations you feel are appropriate.

Incident Reports

Beyond the essential information, there will be times when it is appropriate to make note of a particular incident or situation and include that information in the child's file.

Incident report forms can also be tools to keep parents informed and to document the fact that you properly notified the child's parent or guardian when an injury or illness requiring professional medical attention occurred. Injury reports in particular will help you identify patterns and help you develop prevention programs.

Smart Tip
Store daily attendance records, including the times of arrival and departure, for at least 90 days.

Tip...

Thorough records will also help you recognize the signs of child abuse at home. Some of the most common types of incident forms are:

- *Illness.* When a child becomes ill while in your care, record the date and time of onset, a description of the symptoms, the response of the staff to the symptoms, who was notified (parent, legal guardian, nurse, physician) and their response.

- *Injury.* When an injury requiring first aid or medical attention occurs in a commercially located center, complete a report that includes the following information:
  a) Name, gender, and age of the injured person
  b) Date and time of the injury
  c) Location where injury occurred
  d) Description of how the injury occurred
  e) Part(s) of the body involved
  f) Description of any consumer product involved
  g) Name of the staff member responsible for the care of the injured person at the time of the incident
  h) Action taken on behalf of the injured following the injury
  i) Name of person who completed the report
  j) Name and address of the facility

- If you run a family child-care center, your report should include the following information:
  a) Name, gender, and age of the injured person
  b) Date and time of the injury
  c) Location where injury occurred
  d) Description of how the injury occurred
  e) Part(s) of the body involved
  f) Action taken on behalf of the injured following the injury

Make three copies of the report: one to give to the child's parents, one to keep in the child's file, and one kept in a chronological injury log as required by your state's law. For an example of an injury report form, turn to page 170 in Chapter 15.

Child Information Sheet

Child's name (last, first, middle) _____

Parent/guardian (father) _____

Address _____ Phone _____

Employer _____ Phone _____

Address _____

Parent/guardian (mother)_____

Address _____ Phone _____

Employer _____ Phone _____

Address _____

Special contact information for parents/guardian _____

Child's physician _____ Phone _____

Address _____

Health insurance plan _____

Date of last physical examination* _____

Does your child have any special health problems or medical conditions that require special care? _____

Vaccination status _____

If parents cannot be contacted in an emergency, contact:

Name _____ Relationship to child _____

Address _____ Phone _____

Name _____ Relationship to child _____

Address _____ Phone _____

List every person, including parents, who may pick the child up:

1. _____

2. _____

3. _____

4. _____

Child Information Sheet, continued

Is anyone specifically denied permission to see the child?

_____

Does your child have any unusual eating habits or food preferences or dislikes? (describe)

_____

Is your child toilet-trained? _____

Does your child need assistance with:

❑ Dressing or undressing   ❑ Washing   ❑ Eating   ❑ Toileting

Does your child usually nap?_____

Time of day _____How long? _____

Does your child have any special problems or fears?_____

_____

What are your child's interests or favorite acitivities?_____

_____

Other children living at home:

Name _____Age _____ Boy/Girl (circle one)

Name _____Age _____ Boy/Girl (circle one)

Name _____Age _____ Boy/Girl (circle one)

Name _____Age _____ Boy/Girl (circle one)

Other information that might assist the center's staff in understanding and caring for the child:

_____

_____

_____

_____

_____

*Any child who has not had a well-baby or well-child examination recently (within the past six months for children under two years old and within one year for those two to six years old) should be exained within 30 days of admission to this facility.

- *Misconduct.* When children have serious behavior problems, you need to notify their parents, as well as establish a record of the situation in case you decide to expel the youngster. A misconduct report can be a simple form listing the name of the child; the date, time, and nature of the incident; the disciplinary action taken; a place for the caregiver to sign; and a place for the parent to acknowledge receipt of the report.

> **Smart Tip**
>
> Complete, current records are important for you to maintain your status as a licensed center. Also, if you ever have a situation that results in a lawsuit, well-kept records will be key to your defense.

- *Other.* Make a record of any other events relating to health and safety, such as a lost child.

Management Records

Keep records on your general operations. Certainly, you'll want to study your financial reports on a regular (at least monthly) basis, but for the numbers to make sense, you need to track other performance elements.

Mitten Rosenberry requires the administrator at each of her centers to complete a weekly report. It tracks daily attendance, the number of telephone inquiries and tours given to prospective customers, the number of new children enrolled, the highlights of the week, and any areas that need improvement. For an example, turn to page 33. Administrators also complete weekly marketing and payroll reports.

Purchasing and Inventory

Your inventory will most likely be limited to the supplies you consume in the process of caring for children, so inventory management will not be the same challenge it is for a retailer or a manufacturer. Even so, you need to keep track of what you buy and use, and what you have on hand.

It's also important to keep track of what you spend. Maintain a file of receipts and other evidence (such as canceled checks and credit card charges) of money spent for food and supplies.

Shop smart. Just because your business expenses are deductible doesn't mean you shouldn't insist on the best deal in terms of both quality and price. Wholesale buying clubs and catalogs often offer the best deals, especially when buying in bulk. If you have time, you may find toys, furnishings, and supplies at garage sales. Trade shows can also

▲

be a great place to shop; many exhibitors offer show discounts and will even sell their displays at the end of a show.

Store supplies in a central location that is cool, dry, and away from strong, direct sunlight. Be sure to rotate your stock, using supplies in a first-in, first-out order. Chapters 7, 8, and 9 discuss specific items you'll need to maintain in inventory.

Programs

This book is about the business side of running a child-care service and is not designed to instruct you on how to develop programs for the children. But it is important that you do indeed have programs; you're not running a baby-sitting service where children are playing alone or watching television all day. You will need to understand children's developmental stages and needs. Plan a variety of activities that are not only fun, but that will encourage development, learning, and social skills.

Most children prefer predictable routines rather than a constantly changing schedule; it's best to do specific activities at the same time every day or on the same day every week.

At the same time, special activities will enrich the children's experience, give staff and children alike a pleasant change from the usual routine, and serve as a selling point for your center. Such special activities that could be done with some regularity include show-and-tell sessions, special games or types of art projects, and other activities that are too difficult or time-consuming to put on the daily schedule.

Other special activities might include holiday-themed events, such as a Halloween costume day, a Valentine exchange, and seasonal activities such as a summer field trip to the zoo. These activities should be planned well in advance and displayed on a monthly calendar in the lobby so that parents can see upcoming events. Field trips will require particular advance work, including obtaining permission slips (see example on page 35), and arranging transportation, but they can uplift the image of quality and interest in the children that you want to project. And they're fun for the caregivers as well as for the children.

Srabian does age-appropriate crafts with her children daily, and she stresses the importance of keeping the projects within the capabilities of the youngsters. "Anything else turns into my project, and then it's no fun to give it to their parents," she says. For special occasions, such as Mother's Day, the kids gather in the kitchen to bake brownies or cookies, which are then

Bright Idea

Set up a set of alphabetical file folders or small "mailboxes" for each client family. You can use this for relaying information about the children and activities, and parents can use it to make payments or return forms.

Weekly Reporting Form

Center:				Date:		
Total Enrollement:						
Average Daily Attendance:						
Actual Daily Attendance:						

Staff Total	Class	Monday	Tuesday	Wednesday	Thursday	Friday
	Infants					
	Total					
	Toddler					
	Toddler					
	Total					
	Preschool 1					
	Preschool 2					
	Total					
	Pre-K 1					
	Pre-K 2					
	Total					
	Kindergarten					
	School-age					
	Total					
	Grand total					

Weekly Reporting Form, continued

Highlights of the week:	Areas that need improvement:
	Steps taken:
Staffing action:	**Staff changes:** (birthdays, positions needed, new employees, resignations, terminations, etc.)
New students:	Withdrawn students and why:
How many children have enrolled from previous tours this month?	How many tours were given last month?
How many children do you have on your waiting list?	What ages?

Travel and Activity Authorization for Family Child-Care Center

I give permission for my child _____ to leave the
[child's full name]

home of _____ with supervision
[name of child-care provider]

for trips in a car, on public transportation to special places, walks to the park, shopping trips, etc. I understand that a certified car seat will be used on all car trips.

Restrictions on trips:

_____

_____

_____

_____

Signature of parent or guardian _____ Date_____

decorated and sent home to the parents. At Easter, the kids dye eggs and make cards for their parents. She also takes her kids on walks and to neighborhood parks.

Accreditation for Family Child-Care Centers

In the past, family child care has been a largely invisible industry, seriously fragmented and lacking any significant degree of networking and support opportunities. But in recent years, a professional development movement has emerged. Providers are rejecting the role of "baby-sitter" and positioning themselves as professionals who offer quality care and developmental guidance to children.

If you are operating a family child-care center at home, you may want to pursue accreditation by the National Association for Family Child Care (NAFCC), a national membership organization that works with more than 400 state and local family child-care associations across the United States (see Appendix). NAFCC developed its first accreditation system in 1988 and implemented a new, more specialized system in 1999.

NAFCC accreditation standards cover these content areas: relationships, environment, activities, developmental learning goals, safety and health, and professional business practices. A study conducted by the Families and Work Institute confirmed that accreditation increases providers' professionalism and self-esteem, improves the quality of care, and develops leadership skills. The study revealed ten specific reasons why providers like accreditation:

Bright Idea
Online discussion groups can be a wealth of information for child-care providers. Participants discuss a wide range of issues, from children's behavior to business management. You can learn, share, and be assured you're not the only one with a particular problem.

1. Providers learn from the accreditation process. Accredited providers, even those with years of experience and graduate degrees in early childhood education, found that accreditation is not just a "seal of approval." It also gave them the opportunity to examine their homes and programs and provided an incentive to improve.

2. Accreditation increases providers' self-esteem. Accredited providers said that having a national organization confirm that they operate in a professional manner boosts their self-esteem and makes parents feel good about who they are trusting to care for their children.

3. It makes providers feel more professional. Accreditation makes providers feel like what they're doing is something special and is not simply baby-sitting or something that just anyone could do well.

4. It gives providers a more concrete definition of quality in family child care. Accreditation describes concrete components of quality that are specific to family child care, not a commercial child-care center.

5. It keeps providers excited about their work. Accredited providers report that the accreditation process helps revitalize them and keeps their jobs challenging.

6. It encourages providers to pursue ongoing training and support. Accreditation gives providers a successful self-study experience and frequently leads to more training and participation in local professional associations.

7. It promotes higher quality than state regulations require. Most state regulations address minimal health and safety standards; accreditation represents a higher level of quality.

8. Accredited providers become leaders in the field. Accreditation can be a stepping stone to greater involvement in family child-care issues at the local, state, or national level.

9. Accreditation helps providers market their programs to parents. The process of accreditation creates additional value in a provider's program when it's explained to parents.

10. It helps some providers earn more money. Accredited providers often see their revenue increase because they are better able to communicate with parents and are more likely to get paid by all their clients on time and keep all their spaces filled. Some accredited providers raise their fees because they feel more confident about the quality of their programs.

Are You on a Mission?

At any given moment, most child-care providers have a very clear understanding of the mission of their company. It may not be written down, but they know what they are doing, how and where it's being done, and who their customers are. Some of the operators I talked with didn't have a formal written mission statement, some did, but all could clearly and concisely articulate their mission when asked.

If you're a solo operator and want to stay small, it's probably enough for you to keep your mission statement in your head. But if you have employees and want to eventually become a large company, it will help if you are guided by a written mission statement that can be easily communicated to others.

A mission statement defines what an organization is and why it exists. Writing it down and communicating it to others creates a sense of commonality and a more coherent approach to what you're trying to do.

Even in a very small organization, a written mission statement helps everyone involved see the big picture and keeps them focused on the true goals of the business. At a minimum, your mission statement should define who your primary customers are, identify the products and services you offer, and describe the geographical location in which you operate.

A mission statement should be short—usually just one sentence and certainly no more than two. A good idea is to cap it at 100 words. Anything longer than that isn't a mission statement and will probably confuse your employees.

Once you have articulated your message, communicate it as often as possible to everyone in the company, along with customers and suppliers. Post it on the wall, hold meetings to talk about it, and include a reminder of the statement in employee correspondence.

It's more important to adequately communicate the mission statement to employees than to customers. It's not uncommon for an organization to try to use a mission statement primarily for promotion and secondarily to help employees identify what business they're in, but that doesn't work very well. The most effective mission statements are developed strictly for internal communication and discussion. Your mission statement doesn't have to be clever or catchy—just accurate.

And though your mission statement may never win an advertising or creativity award, it can still be a very effective customer relations tool. One idea is to print your

▲

mission statement on a poster-sized panel, have every employee sign it and hang it in a prominent place so parents and even the children can see it. You can also include it on your brochures and invoices.

Mitten Rosenberry's mission statement reads: "To provide high-quality programming in an innovative environment that supports the family, respects the child, builds character, and

> **Bright Idea**
>
> Review your mission statement once a year. Make sure it still accurately reflects your operation and your goals, and revise it if necessary.

encourages learning through exploration." She says that statement is the foundation on which all programming and environment decisions are made.

Janet Hale's mission statement is similar: "The purpose of [the child-care facility] is to promote quality child care to Exeter and the outlying areas with a program conducive to emotional, educational, physical, and social development. It is our intent to provide a complete educational curriculum suited to the age and maturity of each child, as well as an environment that leads to the well-rounded growth of all children." Hale says the statement is used as a tool in staff meetings to guide plans and programs.

Though Suzanne Wright doesn't have a document labeled "mission statement," she provides parents with a statement about her operation and philosophy. In part, it reads: "My main teaching concern for young children is to teach them social skills such as how to have fun together without physical or verbal hurting of each other. I also emphasize good manners, safety, and following directions. I am consistent with the rules and offer enough structure so that the children feel secure in their surroundings and daily activities."

To help you write your mission statement, use the "Mission Statement Worksheet" on page 39. Then get to work.

Mission Statement Worksheet

To develop an effective mission statement, ask yourself these questions:

○ Why does my company exist? Who do we serve? What is our purpose?

_____

_____

_____

_____

○ What are our strengths, weaknesses, opportunities, and threats?

_____

_____

_____

_____

○ Considering the above, along with our expertise and resources, what business should we be in?

_____

_____

_____

_____

○ What is important to us? What do we stand for?

_____

_____

_____

_____

Now that you've answered those questions, you are ready to write your own mission statement. Use the area below.

_____

_____

_____

_____

_____

_____

_____

Structuring
Your Business

There's a lot more to starting a child-care service than loving kids and having a big box of toys. This chapter will discuss the various issues you need to consider when you're setting up.

Whether your goal is a one-person family child-care operation, a small, commercially located center, or a national chain, you need to start with a written business plan. This helps you think through what you're doing, see your strengths and weaknesses, and figure out a way to overcome challenges on paper before you actually have to face them in real life. Writing a business plan is not just an unpleasant but necessary chore; it creates the foundation and sets the vision of your company.

Your business plan should include worst-case scenarios. You'll benefit from thinking ahead about what you'll do if things don't go as you want them to. Think about things such as equipment breakdowns, employees who don't show up (even for valid reasons), parents who don't pay, children who get sick or injured, and other challenges that are simply a part of doing business today.

Naming Your Company

Your company name can be an important marketing tool. A well-chosen name can work very hard for you; an ineffective name means you have to work much harder at marketing your firm and letting people know what you have to offer.

Your company name should very clearly identify what you do in a way that will appeal to your target market. It should be short, catchy, and memorable—and even cute is acceptable in this industry. Janet Hale's stepmother suggested Gingerbread House for her business because she thought it was cute. Hale agreed, and the name has worked well. The name you choose should also be easy to pronounce and spell—people who can't say your company name may use you, but they won't refer you to anyone else. And it's a good idea for the name to be something small children can manage to say. If you are a small, family child-care provider, you may decide that your business doesn't even need a name, as did Suzanne Wright. Take a systematic approach to naming your company. Once you've decided on two or three possibilities, take the following steps.

- *Check the name for effectiveness and functionality.* Does it quickly and easily convey what you do? Is it easy to say and spell? Is it memorable in a positive way? Ask several of your friends and associates to serve as a focus group to help you evaluate the name's impact.

- *Search for potential conflicts in your local market.* Find out if any other local or regional business serving your market area has a name so similar that yours might confuse the public.

- *Check for legal availability.* Exactly how you do this depends on the legal structure you choose. Typically, sole proprietorships and partnerships operating under a name other than that of the owner(s) are required by the county, city, or state to register their fictitious name. Even if it's not required, it's a good idea, because that means no one else can use that name.

Corporations usually operate under their corporate name. In either case, you need to check with the appropriate regulatory agency to be sure the name you choose is available.

- *Check for use on the internet.* If someone else is already using your name as a domain on the web, consider coming up with something else. Even if you have no intention of developing a web site of your own, the use could be confusing to your customers.

- *Check to see if the name conflicts with any name listed on your state's trademark register.* Your state Department of Commerce can either help you or direct you to the correct agency. You should also check with the trademark register maintained by the U.S. Patent and Trademark Office (PTO).

Once the name you've chosen passes these tests, you need to protect it by registering it with the appropriate state agency; again, your state Department of Commerce can help you. Though most independent child-care centers are local operations, if you expect to be doing business on a national level, you should also register the name with the PTO. Lois Mitten Rosenberry in Toledo, Ohio, learned this lesson the hard way. The first name she chose for her centers was taken; the name she finally came up with was available in Ohio, but two years later, a national chain using that name formed in another state. So as she expands outside of Ohio, she has had to develop a new name and tag line, which she has registered.

Choosing a Legal Structure

One of the first decisions you'll need to make about your new business is the legal structure of your company. This is an important decision, and it can affect your financial liability, the amount of taxes you pay, the degree of ultimate control you have over the company, as well as your ability to raise money, attract investors, and ultimately sell the business. However, legal structure shouldn't be confused with operating structure. Attorney Robert S. Bernstein, managing partner with the Bernstein Law Firm PC, explains the difference: "The legal structure is the ownership structure—who actually owns the company. The operating structure defines who makes management decisions and runs the company."

A sole proprietorship is owned by the proprietor; a partnership is owned by the partners; and a corporation is owned by the shareholders. Another business structure is the

Beware!

Be sure to check the zoning of any location before signing a lease to make sure you can operate a child-care center there. Don't assume that just because you're in a commercial site, you can get a license. Toledo, Ohio, child-care provider Lois Mitten Rosenberry says every time she has opened a new center, she's had to get a special use permit.

limited liability company (LLC), which combines the tax advantages of a sole proprietorship with the liability protection of a corporation. The rules on LLCs vary by state; check with your state's Department of Corporations for the latest requirements.

Sole proprietorships and partnerships can be operated however the owners choose. In a corporation, the shareholders typically elect directors, who in turn elect officers, who then employ other people to run and work in the company. But it's entirely possible for a corporation to have only one shareholder and to essentially function as a sole proprietorship. In any case, how you plan to operate the company should not be a major factor in your choice of legal structures. Rather, the decision should be made based on tax and liability issues.

So what goes into choosing a legal structure? The first point, says Bernstein, is who is actually making the decision on the legal structure. If you're starting the company by yourself, you don't need to take anyone else's preferences into consideration. "But if there are multiple people involved, you need to consider how you're going to relate to each other in the business," he says. "You also need to consider the issue of asset protection and limiting your liability in the event things don't go well."

Something else to think about is your target customers and what their perceptions will be of your structure. While it's not necessarily true, Bernstein says, "There is a tendency to believe that the legal form of a business has some relationship to the sophistication of the owners, with the sole proprietor as the least sophisticated and the corporation as the most sophisticated." The children won't care, but you may find that you command more respect from their parents and the community if you have "Inc." after your company name.

Your image notwithstanding, the biggest advantage of forming a corporation is in the area of asset protection, which, says Bernstein, is the process of making sure that the assets you don't want to put into the business don't stand liable for the business's debt. However, to take advantage of the protection a corporation offers, you must respect the corporation's identity. That means maintaining the corporation as a separate entity; keeping your corporate and personal funds separate, even if you are the sole shareholder; and following your state's rules regarding holding annual meetings and other record-keeping requirements.

Is any one of these structures better than another? No. Child-care businesses operate as sole proprietorships, partnerships, and corporations, and they made their choices based on what was best for their particular situation, which is what you should do. For example, Mitten Rosenberry has incorporated but is the sole stockholder. Hale started as a sole proprietor in Exeter, California, opened her first commercial center in a partnership arrangement and has since incorporated. "Being in a partnership and even 50 percent shareholders is like being married," she observes. "Everything is a negotiation. But we take the best of me and the best of her, and what we get is a center that is, hopefully, the best."

Do you need an attorney to set up a corporation or a partnership? Again, no. Bernstein says there are plenty of good do-it-yourself books and kits on the market, and most of the state agencies that oversee corporations have guidelines you can use. Even so, it's always a good idea to have a lawyer at least look over your documents before you file them, just to make sure they are complete and will allow you to truly function as you want to.

Finally, remember that your choice of legal structure is not an irrevocable decision, although if you're going to make a switch, it's easier to go from the simpler forms to the more sophisticated ones than the other way around. Bernstein says the typical pattern is to start as a sole proprietor and then move up to a corporation as the business grows. But if you need the asset protection of a corporation from the beginning, start out that way. Says Bernstein, "If you're going to the trouble to start a business, decide on a structure and put it all together. It's worth the extra effort to make sure it's really going to work."

Licenses and Permits

The specific licenses and permits you'll need will vary by state, sometimes even by municipality, and may differ depending on whether you are homebased or in a commercial facility, and whether or not you offer transportation in your service package.

Your local business licensing agency should be able to tell you what types of licenses you'll need and where to get them. You should also contact your state agency that regulates child-care centers; they often go by various names, but your state information office should be able to direct you to the right department. If you have access to the internet, note that the National Child Care Information Center profiles each state's information on its web site at www.nccic.org.

In most communities, family child-care providers—that is, providers working in their homes—are required to be licensed by or registered with the appropriate county or state government agency. The process is generally not complicated, and the details vary by jurisdiction. You may be required to complete a training program, and the agency may send an inspector out to check your home to be sure you have the necessary facilities to provide a safe, secure environment for children.

Maintain and display in one central area current copies of applicable licenses, inspection reports, and documentation that all required corrections have been completed. This allows parents, staff, and visitors to assess the extent of evaluation and compliance of your facility with regulatory and voluntary requirements. Though specific documents vary by state, the items you display may include:

- Licensing/registration reports
- Fire inspection reports
- Sanitation inspection reports
- Building code inspection reports
- Plumbing, gas, and electrical inspection reports
- Zoning inspection reports
- Results of all water tests
- Evacuation drill records
- Any accreditation certificates

Trademark and Copyright Issues

It's very important to understand and respect trademarks and copyrights as you design and operate your child-care business. These come under the legal definition of intellectual property, and litigation over unauthorized and inappropriate use of intellectual property is on the rise.

Exactly what is a trademark? According to the PTO, "A trademark includes any word, name, symbol, or device, or any combination, used, or intended to be used, in commerce to identify and distinguish the goods of one manufacturer or seller from goods manufactured or sold by others, and to indicate the source of the goods. In short, a trademark is a brand name."

A trademark can be tremendously valuable to the company that owns it, and most go to great lengths to control how their trademarks are used. For example, you can buy posters with Disney characters to frame and hang on your walls, but if you hire an artist to paint Cinderella or Mickey Mouse on your walls, you may well find yourself the recipient of a cease-and-desist letter from The Walt Disney Co.—as a child-care center in Ft. Lauderdale, Florida, found out the hard way.

If you come up with a clever name or logo for your child-care business, it may be worth your while to trademark it. While registering your trademark is not essential, it does offer some benefits. It gives notice to the public of your claim of ownership of the mark, a legal presumption of ownership nationwide, and the exclusive right to use the mark on or in connection with the goods or services set forth in the registration.

In the business world, there are plenty of horror stories about people who named their business but didn't bother to register that name with the PTO, and were later forced to change the name because someone else decided to use and register it. You can access information about the process of applying for trademark protection and patents via the PTO's web site or by contacting the PTO by phone (see Appendix).

Once you have established a trademark, you must use it, or you risk losing it. Trademarks not actively used for two or more years may be considered abandoned—which means someone else can begin using the mark, and you will have no recourse.

You also need to control your mark. Do not allow others to use your mark without your consent or without restricting what product or service it represents. Think about how companies such as McDonald's and The Walt Disney Company aggressively challenge unauthorized use of their trademarks. They understand how much they have to lose if they fail to control their marks.

If you discover someone using your mark without your authorization, consult with an attorney to determine the most appropriate and effective action.

In general, copyrights protect written material from unauthorized use. Don't reproduce copyrighted items (pages from books, magazines, etc., or music) without permission or without paying for the right to do so.

Insurance

A smart approach to obtaining insurance for your business is to find an agent who works with other child-care businesses. The agent should be willing to help you analyze your needs, evaluate the risks you're willing to accept and the risks you need to insure against, and work with you to keep your insurance costs down.

Insurance companies often stipulate compliance with health and safety regulations before issuing or continuing a policy, which reduces your risks. Some will even assist you with risk management consulting. Remember, insurance will take care of the financial loss associated with a covered incident, accident, or injury, but it can't erase the pain and inconvenience. Though you need to have insurance, your goal should be to never file a claim.

If you are working from your home, be aware that your basic homeowners policy does not automatically cover your business assets and activities—in fact, most exclude certain types of home business claims, especially if they are related to a child-care service. Some insurance companies will decline claims related to your business if they find out you have been operating a business at home without informing them. Also, your homeowners insurance carrier may decline to renew your policy if it becomes aware that you have been providing child care without special coverage. The best approach is one that is honest and upfront. There are plenty of small-business insurance packages that are sold separately or as add-ons to homeowners policies, that provide adequate coverage for both property and liability. Use the "Insurance Policy Evaluation Worksheet" starting on page 50 to assess different policies.

It's a good idea to discuss your insurance coverage with the parents of children in your care. They should know what your insurance covers, especially if you are considering your insurance costs when setting rates.

The basic types of business insurance you need are:

- Accident insurance on children
- Liability insurance
- Vehicle insurance on any kind of vehicle owned or leased by the facility and used to transport children
- Property insurance
- Workers' compensation insurance (if you have employees)

> **Tip...**
>
> ## Smart Tip
>
> When you purchase insurance on your equipment and inventory, ask what documentation the insurance company will require before you have to file a claim. That way, you will be sure to maintain appropriate records, and the claims process will be easier if it is ever necessary.

Accident Insurance

Accident, or medical, insurance on the children enrolled in your center pays for their doctor and hospital bills if they are injured while in your care. Most liability policies include medical and accident coverage. If yours does not, you may want to purchase separate coverage.

> **Tip...**
>
> ## Smart Tip
>
> Sit down with your insurance agent every year and review your insurance needs. As your company grows, your insurance needs are sure to change. Also, insurance companies are always developing new products to meet the needs of the growing homebased and small-business market, and it's possible one of these new policies is appropriate for you.

Liability Insurance

The greatest risk you'll face as a child-care provider is the injury or death of a child in your care. If you are sued and found to be responsible, you could lose a great deal of money and even personal assets not related to your business. Liability insurance can protect you by paying expenses, damages, judgments, and your defense costs up to the limits of the policy.

Professional Advisors

As a business owner, you may be the boss, but you can't be expected to know everything. You will occasionally need to turn to professionals for information and assistance. It's a good idea to establish relationships with these professionals before you get into a crisis situation.

To shop for a professional service provider, ask your friends and associates for recommendations. You might also check with your local chamber of commerce or trade association for referrals. Find someone who understands your industry and specific business and appears eager to work with you. Check them out with the Better Business Bureau and the appropriate state licensing agency before committing yourself.

Beware!
Some child-care providers try to substitute liability waivers signed by parents for adequate insurance coverage. Legal experts agree that waivers typically do not hold up in court. A waiver will not prevent you from being sued or held financially responsible if a child is injured at your center.

As a child-care service owner, the professional service providers you're likely to need include:

- *Attorney*. You need a lawyer who practices in the area of business law, is honest, and appreciates your patronage. In most parts of the United States, there are many lawyers who are willing to compete fiercely for the privilege of serving you. Interview several and choose one you feel comfortable with. Be sure to clarify the fee schedule ahead of time, and get your agreement in writing. Keep in mind that good commercial lawyers don't come cheap; if you want good advice, you must be willing to pay for it. Your attorney should review all contracts, leases, letters of intent, and other legal documents before you sign them. This person can also help you collect bad debts and establish personnel policies and procedures. Of course, if you are unsure of the legal ramifications of any situation, call your attorney immediately.

- *Accountant*. Among your outside advisors, your accountant is likely to have the greatest impact on the success or failure of your business. If you are forming a corporation, your accountant should counsel you on tax issues during startup. On an ongoing basis, your accountant can help your organize the statistical data concerning your business, assist in charting future actions based on past performance, and advise you on your overall financial strategy regarding purchasing, capital investment, and other matters related to your business goals. A good accountant will also serve as a tax advisor, making sure you are in compliance with all applicable regulations and that you don't overpay any taxes.

Insurance Policy Evaluation Worksheet

Get answers to these questions for every policy you consider before making a final purchase decision.

Policy type _____

Company name _____

Agent name _____

1. How does the company limit its risks?

   Maximum number of children? _____

   License, registration, or certification required? _____

   Professional association membership/accreditation required/considered? ____

   _____

   Other underwriting guidelines/considerations (pools, fences, pets, security, etc.)

   _____

   _____

2. What is and is not covered? _____

   _____

   Activities away from the home or center? _____

   Transporting children? _____

   Physical, sexual, or mental abuse? _____

   Food service? _____

   Employee conduct? _____

   Administering medications? _____

   Other activities/conditions: _____

   _____

3. What are the liability and accident insurance (medical payment) limits?

   Per claim? _____

   Per year? _____

Insurance Policy Evaluation Worksheet, continued

4. What is the deductible? _____

5. What is the premium? _____

6. Is the policy an occurrence form or a claims-made form? _____

_____

7. What is the company's reputation? What information came from:

   Best's Insurance Reports _____

   State Department of Insurance _____

   Consumer Reports _____

   Government agencies _____

   Professional associations _____

   Business colleagues _____

   Friends _____

   Personal experience _____

8. What is the procedure for filing claims?

   _____

   _____

9. Does the company offer other types of coverage, and will additional policies receive multiple policyholder discounts?

   _____

   _____

10. Is the agent knowledgeable and helpful?

   _____

   _____

You'd Better Shop Around

Buying insurance is a complex and challenging process. Don't rush through it; failing to understand your coverage now could haunt you if you have a problem in the future.

○ *Evaluate all your options before making any decisions.* Don't buy the first policy just because it seems to offer everything you need.

○ *Ask the same questions about each policy.* Make notes so you can compare all the policies on an apples-to-apples basis. Use the "Insurance Policy Evaluation Worksheet" starting on page 50.

○ *Don't be afraid or embarrassed to ask questions.* Be certain you understand exactly what is and is not covered by each policy, even if it means repeating your questions or asking the agent to rephrase answers. If you feel the agent is not sufficiently knowledgeable about insurance for child-care providers, ask to speak to someone who is.

○ *Take your time.* Don't give in to sales pressure to buy before you are ready. In fact, if you feel pressured by an agent, consider buying elsewhere.

- *Insurance agent.* A good independent insurance agent can assist you with all aspects of your business insurance, from general liability to employee benefits, and probably even handle your personal lines as well. Look for an agent who works with a wide range of insurers and understands the child-care business. This agent should be willing to explain the details of various types of coverage, consult with you to determine the most appropriate coverage, help you understand the degree of risk you are taking, work with you in developing risk-reduction programs, and assist in expediting any claims.

- *Banker.* You need a business bank account and a relationship with a banker. Don't just choose the bank you've always done your personal banking with; it may not be the best bank for your business. Interview several bankers before making a decision on where to place your business. Once your account is opened, maintain a relationship with the banker. Periodically sit down and review your accounts and the services you use to make sure you are getting the package most appropriate for your situation. Ask for advice if you have financial questions or problems. When you need a loan or a bank reference to provide to creditors, the relationship you have established will work in your favor.

- *Consultants.* The consulting industry is booming, and for good reason. Consultants can provide valuable, objective input on all aspects of your business.

Consider hiring a business consultant to evaluate your business plan or a marketing consultant to assist you in that area. There are consultants who specialize in various aspects of child care and early childhood education. When you are ready to hire employees, a human resources consultant may help you avoid some costly mistakes. Consulting fees vary widely, depending on the individual's experience, location, and field of expertise. If you can't afford to hire a consultant, consider contacting the business school at the nearest college or university and hiring an MBA student to help you.

Bright Idea

Protect your own personal income with disability insurance. According to the Social Security Administration, a 20-year-old worker has a 3 in 10 chance of becoming disabled before reaching retirement age. The nature of the work you do puts you at greater risk for injury than many other occupations. What will happen to you and your family if you are unable to work due to a short- or long-term disability?

- *Computer expert.* You'll use a computer to manage your business and may even have computers in your facility for the children to use. Your computer and data are extremely valuable assets, so if you don't know much about computers, you should find someone to help you select a system and the appropriate software, and to be available to help you maintain, troubleshoot, and expand your system as you need it.

Most business owners we talked with have ongoing relationships with accountants and know of an attorney they can call on if they need one. They also have other advisors.

Create Your Own Advisory Board

Not even the president of the United States is expected to know everything. That's why he surrounds himself with advisors—experts in particular areas who provide knowledge and information to help him make decisions. Savvy small-business owners use a similar strategy.

You can assemble a team of volunteer advisors to meet with you periodically to offer advice and direction. Because this isn't an official or legal entity, you have a great deal of latitude in how you set it up. Advisory boards can be structured to help with the direct operation of your company and to keep you informed on various business, legal, and financial trends that may affect you. Use these tips to set up your advisory board:

- *Structure a board that meets your needs.* Generally, you'll want a legal advisor, an accountant, a marketing expert, a human resources person, an expert in early child development and/or education, and perhaps a financial advisor. You may also want successful entrepreneurs from other industries who understand the basics of business and will view your operation with a fresh eye.

- *Ask the most successful people you can find, even if you don't know them well.* You'll be surprised at how willing people are to help another business succeed.

- *Be clear about what you are trying to do.* Let your prospective advisors know what your goals are and that you don't expect them to take on an active management role or to assume any liability for your company or for the advice they offer.

Beware!

Not all attorneys are created equal, and you may need more than one. For example, the lawyer who can best guide you in contract negotiations may not be the most effective counsel when it comes to employment issues. Ask about areas of expertise and specialization before retaining a lawyer.

- *Don't worry about compensation.* Advisory board members are rarely compensated with more than lunch or dinner. Of course, if members of your board provide a direct service—for example, if an attorney reviews a contract or an accountant prepares a financial statement—then they should be paid at their normal rate. But that's not part of their job as an advisory board member. Keep in mind that, even though you don't write them a check, your advisory board members will likely benefit in a variety of tangible and nontangible ways. Being on your board will expose them to ideas and perspectives they may not otherwise see and will also expand their own network.

- *Consider group dynamics when holding meetings.* You may want to meet with all the members together, or in small groups of one or two. It all depends on how they relate to each other and what you need to accomplish.

- *Ask for honesty, and don't be offended when you get it.* Your pride might be hurt when someone points out something you are doing wrong, but the awareness will be beneficial in the long run.

- *Learn from failure as well as success.* Encourage board members to tell you about their mistakes so you can avoid making them.

- *Respect the contribution your board members are making.* Let them know you appreciate how busy they are, and don't abuse or waste their time.

- *Make it fun.* You are, after all, asking these people to donate their time, so create a pleasant atmosphere.

- *Listen to every piece of advice.* Stop talking and listen. You don't have to follow every piece of advice, but you need to hear it.

- *Provide feedback to the board.* Good or bad, let the board know what you did and what the results were.

When she started her company, Mitten Rosenberry knew she needed more business knowledge than she had, so she took a class in small-business financial management at the local university. "It was taught by one of the commercial lending officers at a local bank. He said that most small businesses fail, but the owners who surround themselves with a team of professional advisors will overcome those odds, and their chances of succeeding are much greater," she says. "I wanted to succeed, so I put together an advisory board. They steered me around some bad mistakes I would have made on my own. They have also prodded me on. There were times I didn't want to grow, and they said, 'You're ready.'"

5

Start-Up Economics and Financial Management

The issue of money has two sides: How much do you need to start and operate, and how much can you expect to take in? Doing this analysis is often extremely difficult for small-business owners, most of whom would rather be in the trenches getting the work done than bound to a desk dealing with tiresome numbers.

Financial management is not a one-time, do-it-and-it's-done chore. It's something you'll have to deal with every day. Sometimes the money side of a child-care business can get very emotional; you're providing a service many of your customers view as a necessity, and things can get stressful if they're having trouble paying you.

Taking a serious, professional, businesslike approach to money and financial management is an important part of having a successful, profitable child-care business.

Start-Up Costs: How Much Do You Need?

So what do you need in the way of cash and available credit to open your doors? Depending on what you already own, the services you want to offer and whether you'll be homebased or in a commercial location, that number could range from a few hundred to tens of thousands of dollars.

As you consider your own situation, don't pull a start-up number out of the air; use your business plan to calculate how much you need to start your ideal operation, and then figure out how much you have. If you have all the cash you need, you're very fortunate. If you don't, you need to start playing with the numbers and deciding what you can do without.

Many of the child-care entrepreneurs we talked with used their personal savings and equipment they already owned to start their businesses. Because the start-up costs for a family child-care business are relatively low, you'll find traditional financing difficult to obtain. Banks and other lenders would much rather lend amounts much larger than you'll need and are likely to be able to qualify for. A commercially located center will take a more substantial investment and would likely qualify for a bank loan if you need it.

Suzanne Wright spent several hundred dollars on start-up requirements, including background checks for herself and her husband, fire department inspection fees, and educational requirements, plus feeding chairs, automobile safety seats, cribs, and toys. Christine Srabian started with what she already owned, and added equipment and toys as needed over the years. Janet Hale, owner of Gingerbread House in Exeter, California, spent considerably more—about $5,000—to set up her family child-care center because she remodeled her garage to serve as the primary room for her business as well as added a bathroom for the children. When she opened her first commercial location, she used a combination of personal savings and credit cards to pay the expenses. By the time she opened her second location, she was able to qualify for a commercial loan. Lois Mitten Rosenberry took out a second mortgage on her home to get the $15,000 she needed to adequately equip her first Children's Discovery Center in Toledo in 1982. Doris McNeill traded in her car for a van and was able to get Kids on Wheels open with just a few thousand dollars of her own cash.

As you're putting together your financial plan, consider these sources of start-up funds:

- *Your own resources.* Do a thorough inventory of your assets. People generally have more assets than they immediately realize. This could include savings accounts, equity in real estate, retirement accounts, vehicles, recreation equipment, collections, and other investments. You may opt to sell assets for cash or use them as collateral for a loan. Take a look, too, at your personal line of credit; most of the equipment you'll need is available through retail stores that accept credit cards.

> **Smart Tip**
>
> Rather than appeal to a prospective investor for money, ask him to review your business plan. If he likes the plan, he may offer to invest without you having to ask.

- *Friends and family.* The logical next step after gathering your own resources is to approach your friends and relatives who believe in you and want to help you succeed. Be cautious with these arrangements; no matter how close you are, present yourself professionally, put everything in writing, and be sure the people you approach can afford to take the risk of investing in your business.

- *Partners.* Though most family child-care centers are owned by just one person, you may want to consider using the "strength in numbers" principle and look around for someone who may want to team up with you in your venture. You may choose someone who has financial resources and wants to work side by side with you in the business. Or you may find someone who has money to invest but no interest in doing the actual work. Be sure to create a written partnership agreement that clearly defines your respective responsibilities and obligations.

- *Government programs.* Take advantage of the abundance of local, state, and federal programs designed to support small businesses in general, and child-care programs in particular. Make your first stop the U.S. Small Business Administration; then investigate various other programs. Women, minorities, and veterans should check out niche financing possibilities designed to help these groups get into business. The business section of your local library is a good place to begin your research. Another good resource is your local community child-care resource center; though the names of the organizations and their exact services vary, these agencies can direct you to a variety of sources for financial and other assistance. Janet Hale suggests contacting your state's Department of Education to see if it offers any funding for preschool programs.

Building Banking Relationships

Whether or not you need a start-up loan, you'll need a business bank account and a business relationship with a bank. The nearest bank or the one where you've had your personal account may not be the best choice. Remember, your banker will be one of your most important professional advisors, so shop around, meet with several, find out what they have to offer, and ask them why you should use them.

Of course, if you are looking for a loan, you don't want to walk empty-handed into a bank you've never done business with and ask for a major line of credit. Put together a package that clearly demonstrates to the bank that you are a good credit risk and that it will benefit by establishing a line of credit for you.

In these days of banking mergers and acquisitions, along with personnel turnover, it's a good idea to have relationships with more than one bank. If you have a single line of credit with one bank and that bank is acquired, you could find your line of credit canceled through no fault of your own. Or if you have a strong relationship with a loan officer who gets promoted or transferred or changes jobs, you may find the new loan officer is not as receptive to your needs. Protect yourself by making sure you always have a financial backup.

Setting Prices

The fees you charge will provide the financial base for your company and your income. They need to be competitive in your market, reasonable and affordable for the parents, and also fair to you. You need to consider a variety of issues, including your costs, the profit you want to make, the going rates in your area, and what the families you are targeting can afford. Setting your rates, explaining—and often justifying—them to parents, and then collecting the money are all part of being in the child-care business.

Because you will be offering a carefully planned curriculum that is far more than a mere baby-sitting service, you are justified in establishing a fee structure similar in design to a private school. A one-time enrollment charge of half a week's tuition will hardly raise an eyebrow, but it will fairly compensate you for the cost in time, paperwork, and special attention each entrant needs.

Calculating how much to charge for space in your center will be based primarily on three variables:

1. Labor and materials (or supplies)
2. Overhead
3. Profit

A fourth factor uncommon to most businesses but significant for a child-care center is the limit to the number of children you can accommodate. In most fields, if your business grows, you just keep hiring employees to serve the increasing number of customers. But in child care, state laws

> **Tip...**
>
> ## Smart Tip
> Find out about any child-care subsidy programs in your community that would allow you to serve low-income or other eligible families who may not otherwise be able to afford your rates.

and practical reality limit the number of children you can accept, putting a lid on the income potential of your business. To overcome this, successful child-care operators often open more locations in nearby areas to increase their client base and income.

Labor and Materials

Until you establish records to use as a guide, you must estimate the costs of labor and materials. Labor costs are the wages and benefits you pay your employees. As the owner, your salary (if you don't take your personal income directly from net profit) must be included in the total labor charge. If you make no official allowance for yourself but merely draw from the net profit, you should include your labor, proportionate to your input, in the total labor estimate.

Labor cost is usually expressed as an hourly rate. A little research should give you a good idea of the going rate in your area for different positions. As you calculate your labor costs, remember to include the hidden costs (payroll taxes, benefits, etc.).

To determine the weekly tuition for a full-time attendee, you first have to determine the child-to-caregiver ratio. For purposes of this example, we'll use a 6-to-1 ratio. If the hourly labor cost is $9 (including wages, taxes, and benefits) for one caregiver to watch six children, then the labor cost would be $1.50 per child per hour. You'll have to estimate your materials costs at first; 45 percent of labor is a good average to use until you have a history to measure.

Overhead includes the nonlabor, indirect expenses required to operate your business. If you have past operating expenses to guide you, figuring an overhead rate is not difficult. You simply total all your expenses for one year, excluding labor and materials. Divide this number by your total cost of labor and materials to determine your overhead rate. Of course, at first, you won't have past expenses to guide you, so figure overhead as 30 to 40 percent of your labor-and-materials cost.

Food for Thought

The Child and Adult Care Food Program (CACFP) is a federal program that provides healthy meals and snacks to children and adults receiving day care. CACFP reimburses participating public and private child-care homes and centers for meal costs. Children ages 12 and younger are eligible to receive up to two meals and one snack each day, and after-school care snacks are available to children up to age 18. Eligibility is based on the income level of the child's family. CACFP is a program of the U.S. Department of Agriculture (see Appendix).

Most child-care center operators expect a net profit of 9 to 14 percent of their gross revenue. So let's take a look at how the example works out, assuming that the child will be in your care for 50 hours each week (10 hours a day, 5 days a week):

Labor (50 hours at $1.50 per hour)	$75.00
Materials (45 percent of labor)	$33.75
Total labor and materials	$108.75
Overhead (35 percent of labor and materials)	$38.06
Subtotal	$146.81
Profit (9 percent of $146.81)	$13.21
Weekly tuition	**$160.02**

Round the tuition down to $160 per week.

This is just a basic formula to show you how the calculation is done based on expenses and desired profit. Most child-care centers charge according to the child's age, with parents of children who are not toilet-trained or still prone to "accidents" paying as much as 20 percent more than slightly older children. Very young toddlers and infants also require lower adult-to-child ratios, which raises your labor expenses and contributes to higher fees for toddlers.

The goal in pricing a service is to mark up your labor and materials costs sufficiently to cover overhead expenses and generate sufficient profit. First-time business owners often don't realize that they have priced their services too low.

You may begin the process of determining your prices by using the three elements we just considered, but the only way to judge the viability of that price is to test it in the marketplace. However, even if you find out that other centers are charging less, think carefully before lowering your price. Can you reduce your overhead and maintain profitability? A business that does not earn an adequate profit is more vulnerable to total failure because it does not have the financial cushion that good profits provide.

Also, even though other centers are charging less, your services may be worth more, or those centers may not have any openings, which means that your prospective clients can't place their children there, anyway. Of course, that doesn't necessarily mean families in the area will pay your higher rates; they may not be able to afford to. A

> **Tip...**
>
> **Smart Tip**
>
> Remember the marketing concept of "perceived value" when setting and increasing rates. If you set your fees too low, people may assume your services are not as good as they are at a center that charges more. If you go too high, potential customers may not be able to afford your services. Find a balance that works for you and your market.

little bit of research will tell you what families in your target market are able to pay. In general, families can afford to budget approximately 10 percent of their income for child-care expenses. A check of census data at your library will tell you the income ranges for your community; lower-income families may be eligible for child-care payment assistance.

Take your cost-plus-desired-profit figure and the figure of what families can afford, and see how closely they match. Although you certainly want to be sensitive to a family's budget, keep in mind that it is not your responsibility to help all parents afford child care. Rather, it is your responsibility to set up a quality child-care program based on sound business practices. If you want to serve low-income families, take the time to investigate the various government subsidy programs designed to help people who can't afford to pay the full price of child care. A good place to start is with your local research and referral agency.

Mitten Rosenberry initially set her prices based on the average rates in her community but later increased them on the advice of her advisory board. She realized that if she was going to have the best program in the area, she needed to charge accordingly. "That was hard for me," she admits. "I think people in child care are often reluctant to charge the parents too much. But you have to balance that with the knowledge that if you don't make money, you're not going to stay in business. If you want new equipment, if you want to provide benefits to your staff, if you want to invest in training, you have to have a solid bottom line."

Hourly or Weekly?

You can charge for your services on an hourly, weekly, or even monthly basis. Charging by the hour generally means you are paid only for the time the child is in your care and will not receive any income if the child isn't there. This makes planning your own time and budget more challenging. Weekly or monthly rates based on an anticipated amount of care make more sense and are easier to work with.

You can add an overtime rate to your base rate to accommodate special needs of the parents. Using the example above, you would be charging a parent $160 a week for caring for a child ten hours a day. Let's say the mother typically drops the child off at 7 A.M. and picks him up at 5 P.M. Monday through Friday. But during the first week of every month, the mother's employer asks her to work an extra hour each day, which means she can't pick up the child until 6 P.M. That's an extra five hours for that week when you will be caring for that child, and you can charge an hourly rate for that time. Depending on the circumstances, you may want to calculate the hourly rate based on your standard tuition rate, or you may charge a premium for overtime. In this case, because the extra time is scheduled, you may opt to charge it at "straight time," or $3.20 per hour. Or you may charge it at "time and a half," or $4.80 per hour for the extra five hours over the basic 50 the child is with you.

Increasing Your Revenue

Once you've set your fees and have been operating for a while, you may realize that your income is too low. There are several ways to increase your revenue.

- Charge special fees. You might ask parents to pay for a particular supply or to pay an activity fee to cover the cost of new materials, equipment, special field trips, and/or occasional enrichment activities. If you are a small, family child-care center and have developed a strong relationship with the families whose children you care for, consider asking the parents to pay for the cost of additional training and/or certification for you. Also ask parents to cover the cost of a substitute while you attend this training. Of course, you'll have to help the parents understand how their children will benefit from these fees; if they see an advantage for their children, they will be more likely to accept the extra charges.

- *Change policies.* Your policies can affect the amount of your income. For example, some providers charge an initial registration fee to cover the extra time and materials it takes to register a child. It's acceptable to charge more for infants and toddlers because caring for and supervising them takes more time. Charging a fee when parents are late picking up their children not only raises your income but also reduces the number of late parents. Examine your operation to see where you are providing additional services for the same fee, and consider whether a change in policies that would increase the revenue is appropriate.

- *Increase your rates.* You should increase your basic tuition rate once a year. When you initially register a family, let parents know that your rates will increase somewhat on an annual basis and tell them when they will be notified of the rate changes (usually in the same month each year). Language to this effect should be included in your contract. Give parents ample notice so they can budget for the increase. Announce rate changes in writing to avoid misunderstandings. Your letter might read, "According to our contract, I am to notify you during the month of October about rate increases for the coming year. Beginning January 1, your new weekly rate will be $_____."

Certainly no parent is going to be happy about a rate increase, but they want what is best for their children. Of course, they also want their money's worth, so you need to be prepared to justify any increase. Parents will be more likely to accept higher fees if they understand why they are needed and also see that their child will benefit from them.

To increase parents' understanding, explain how you arrived at your fee. Often, parents do not understand how little family day-care providers make. They typically consider only the amount of income you get and forget to subtract the expenses—and in many cases, they have no idea what expenses you have. You could make up a simple sheet explaining how you determined your new rate.

You could also justify a rate increase by explaining how it will benefit the children in the coming year. For example, if you will be using the revenue generated by a rate increase to purchase new outdoor equipment, provide field trips, or become accredited, explain this to the parents.

Consider this: As you develop professionally, you're worth more, and your rates should increase accordingly. Raise your rates every year, even if it's a very nominal amount. The cost of living goes up; everybody else gets a raise, and so should you.

Tip...

Smart Tip

Don't be afraid to charge penalties for late payments and bad checks, or to ask for cash payment if you get more than one bad check from a parent. You deserve to be paid on time. State your policies and enforce them, and you will rarely have payment problems.

Forms of Payment

You'll receive payments by check and cash, and you may also want to set up a merchant account you can accept credit cards. Check with your bank or the different credit card companies (see Appendix) for information on accepting credit cards. Many child-care and transportation service providers find that automatically debiting a parent's credit card is the easiest and most efficient way to obtain payment. There are fees involved, but many providers find it's worth it. An affordable way to accept credit cards is through an online payment processing service such as PayPal; if you and your clients have PayPal accounts, they can pay you with the credit card of their choice without you needing to have different merchant accounts.

Collection Procedures

Decide when you want payments due, and make that a clear part of your policy statement. At family child-care centers, parents will typically hand the payment to you on the due date when they drop off or pick up their child. In a commercial facility, you might want to have a small facility such as a secure box where parents can quickly drop off their payments without the risk of a check being misplaced because it was casually tossed on the reception desk.

Consider taking an approach similar to this: Send home a late-payment reminder when the payment is two days late (see the example on page 67). If payment is not made within a week, speak to the parents by phone or when they come to drop off or pick up their child. At a predetermined point, you'll have to stop allowing the child (or children) to be dropped off until full payment is made.

You'll also want to establish a schedule of late fees and charges for checks that bounce. Typical fees for late payments range from $5 to $25 per day. For a bad check, be sure you charge enough to cover what your bank charges you, plus a little more for the hassle. Explain your policies to parents at the time of enrollment, and give them a copy of the fees and charges in writing so there is no question later on.

Although you have a right to expect to be paid on time for your services, you might also want to consider ways to make it easy for parents to pay on schedule. Your payment schedule may not match their needs. Some parents will find it

> ### Bright Idea
> If a parent who frequently pays late says the problem is forgetting the check, suggest that they write the check for child care when they get paid. They can keep that check in their wallet or purse and give it to you on the appropriate day. That way, they won't have to remember to write a check each week; you simply remind them it's payday, and they can pull out the check without any further effort.

more convenient to pay you on their payday; others will prefer to pay for two weeks at a time instead of one. If you are having payment problems with a particular parent, find out if a different payment schedule would solve the problem. This may be a little more work for you in terms of bookkeeping, yet it will likely be less of a problem than being paid late every week.

The bulk of your payments will come in on the same day each week, and you should keep this in mind as you plan your record-keeping tasks. Schedule other administrative tasks, such as handling payables and payroll, for days when you won't have a heavy influx of payments.

Keeping Records: Start Right, Stay Right

Regardless of the form of payment—cash, check, or credit card—most of the income you receive from your child-care business will show up on other people's tax returns. Parents use their child-care expenses to determine their allowable child-care credits, and this makes your income very visible to the IRS. Accurate records are vitally important; you must carefully track and report all your income and expenses.

If your business is ever audited, you may find the IRS asking to see documentation such as grocery receipts, copies of menus, and children's attendance records to justify your food purchase deductions. They will also ask to see documentation for automobile use and other expenses. Whatever you spend in the operation of your business is a legitimate deduction, including household child-care supplies such as soap, toilet paper,

paper towels, and tissues; toys and play supplies such as crayons, markers, paint, clay, audiotapes, and videotapes; birthday and holiday gifts to children; educational expenses such as your admission costs for field trips (even though the children's parents have paid for theirs); memberships in child-care organizations; subscriptions to professional journals; and fees for seminars you attend.

Of course, you may not ever be audited, but you'll still benefit from maintaining your records in a way that would make the audit process as painless and efficient as possible. "In the long run, it's easier—and you will always be prepared for whatever happens, whether it's an audit, or whether you need financial documentation for some other purpose," says Vicki L. Helmick, CPA, an accountant in Orlando, Florida.

The first step is to open a separate checking account for your business. "That way, you are not commingling personal and business funds where income or expenses can get lost or miscoded. You will capture your financial information correctly and in one place," Helmick says.

Next, get a business credit card, or at least a separate card in your name that you use exclusively for your child-care business. Charging business expenses will eliminate the risk of losing receipts for cash purchases. Also, Helmick says, if you carry a balance on a credit card that is used solely for business purposes, the interest is deductible; but if you mix business and personal charges on the card, the interest is not even partially deductible.

Late Payment Reminder

Gingerbread House Child-care Centers

Just a reminder: We haven't received your payment!

This is to remind you that your child-care fees for

_____

are now due and payable. Please pay

$_____,

which is due in advance on or before

_____

to avoid further late fees. Thank you!

Courtesy: Gingerbread House

Third, Helmick recommends setting up a good computer-based accounting system; any of the off-the-shelf accounting products will do. Once you are set up, record your information on a timely basis; this is important not only for audits but also so you know how your business is doing in terms of profitability at any given point.

For physical documentation, Helmick suggests designating a filing cabinet for exclusive business use. Set up files by year so it's easy to pull information out by date if necessary. Have separate files for payroll, payables (you may want to set up individual files for each vendor, depending on how many you have), and receivables. Remember that for whatever files you maintain electronically, you must also keep the program so you can access the data—that means keeping software even after you've upgraded.

Beware!

It's possible some of your clients will pay you in cash rather than by check or credit card. You may be tempted to not report this revenue on your income tax return—but don't do it! Failing to report income is a crime and can cost you much more in the long run (in terms of interest, fines, and other civil and criminal penalties) than you might save in the short term. Record and report all your income, no matter how it is received.

Getting Free Supplies and Services

Child-care programs have numerous wants and needs, and you will find that often the easiest way to get what you want is to ask for it. There are many resources willing to donate goods and services, but they have to know what you need.

The first step is to develop a wish list that you can post on a bulletin board or distribute to parents. You might want anything from empty egg cartons or coffee cans for a craft project to a digital camera. You might not get the camera as a gift, but it's possible someone will lend you one for special events—and you'll definitely get the egg cartons and coffee cans.

Here is a sample of some things you might ask for:

- Outgrown clothing and toys
- Used furniture (chairs and couch cushions for a cuddly corner, old mattresses to jump on)
- Holiday decorations
- Plastic dishes and other containers and utensils for sand and water play
- Yarn, needles, and fabric for projects
- Dramatic play props (old clothes, costume jewelry, luggage, etc.)
- Toy and equipment repair services

- Volunteers to help plan, organize, and supervise field trips
- Assistance with craft projects
- Volunteers to share a skill or talent with the children

If parents have items they're not using but you can, most will be happy to donate them to enrich their child's day-care environment. Many may work for companies that have items they would be willing to donate. The key is to make your needs known.

Be sure to show your appreciation to the donors. A simple thank-you note is all that is necessary. Notes written by (or dictated to you and then colored by) the children are appreciated and often cherished by the donors. You might also include a snapshot of the children using the gift. Acknowledge the gifts by posting notices on your bulletin board or including them in your newsletter (if you have one). This not only expresses your appreciation but also may spur others to donate, too.

Locating and
Setting Up

What is the ideal location for your child-
care business? If you want to work from home, the answer to
that question is simple. But if you're opting for a commercial
location, selecting a site takes some serious consideration and
research.

This chapter covers choosing a site and deciding on the basic layout of your facility. The following three chapters discuss the various types of equipment and fixtures you'll need, along with health, safety, and sanitation issues. However, there is a significant amount of overlap in these topics because how rooms will be equipped may affect how you design your floor plan. Read all four of these chapters carefully before you begin shopping for a location or, if you plan to operate from your home, before you begin designing your child-care space.

Choosing a Commercial Location

If you're going to open a center on a commercial site, it makes sense to locate your facility close to your target market. Some parents may prefer a center close to home; others may choose one near their workplace. In the latter case, parents will get to enjoy more time with their children during their morning and evening commutes, as well as have the opportunity to spend time with them during the course of the day, perhaps for lunch or special programs.

Some site suggestions you should consider include:

- A facility within or adjacent to a residential neighborhood or near a school
- A facility in a shopping center where parents with their children are likely to pass by
- Sharing a facility with other community organizations
- Office and planned light industrial parks with a sizable work force

Improving an Existing Facility

Buying or renting a facility that can be converted into a child-care center is usually much more economical than building one from scratch. Some facilities are more conducive to child-care operations than others.

- *Retail conversion.* A vacant retail store with a large parking lot presents an ideal opportunity for a child-care center. A portion of the lot could be fenced as a playground. Because stores typically have little or no interior partitioning, you have tremendous flexibility in designing different play areas, and your staff will be able to see throughout the center from almost anywhere.

Bright Idea

Many large corporations would like to offer on-site child care to their workers. You can approach these companies with a proposal to sublease space within their facility, giving them a significant employee benefit and you a built-in market.

The store will likely have an existing office you can use for your administrative area. Other space may be used for custodian's equipment, kitchen facilities, and perhaps additional restrooms and a laundry room.

- *Converting an apartment building.* Apartment buildings can be successfully converted to accommodate a child-care business, especially buildings with plenty of outside area for a playground. Separate apartments allow for a logical operating plan. The administrative offices, reception area, and supply room can be located in one unit; the kitchen, dining area, and laundry in another; and remaining units can be set up as classrooms and nurseries.

A building with 8 to 12 units should be sufficient, depending on whether the units are one- or two-bedroom apartments. A single-story building is preferable.

Bright Idea

When looking for a commercial site, don't overlook vacant child-care centers. Many business parks and corporate headquarters have facilities for child-care centers that are no longer in use for various reasons (often because a corporation no longer wanted to subsidize the service as a company benefit), but the buildings are designed and equipped for a child-care operation. You could get a great deal on buying or leasing such a facility.

- *Church facilities.* A local church or synagogue may have large education wings that are only used one day each week, usually on weekends. It may be possible to arrange a mutually profitable agreement to use the building's space during the week for your child-care business. It will likely have much of the equipment and fixtures required by your state, which will reduce your start-up expenses.

Be sure your written agreement stipulates that you are merely leasing the space and the business is yours, rather than making yourself an employee of the church. Avoid incorporating the organization's religious philosophy or mission into your operation, as this may limit your market potential to those families in that congregation or of that particular religion. Also include a clause to prevent the church from evicting you and establishing its own day-care center, possibly stealing your clientele and the results of your hard work.

- *House conversion.* A house converted into a commercial child-care center tends to have a reassuring, homelike atmosphere that parents and children find comforting. However, few single-family houses can accommodate a large-scale child-care operation. If your goal is a small operation, a good-sized house with a large, enclosed yard can be ideal. You may need to modify or add restroom facilities to meet state requirements. Also, be sure to check zoning restrictions before you make an investment in the property.

Indoor Space and Equipment

The National Resource Center for Health and Safety in Child Care suggests the following standards for out-of-home child-care programs:

- The designated area for children's activities should contain a minimum of 35 square feet per child, free of furniture and equipment, exclusive of food preparation areas of the kitchen, bathrooms, toilets, areas for the care of ill children, hallways, stairways, laundry, storage, and administrative space. With usual furnishings, this typically amounts to 50 square feet measured wall to wall. Children's behavior tends to be more constructive when sufficient space is available to promote the practice of developmentally appropriate skills. Also, crowding has been associated with an increased risk of developing upper respiratory infections.

- Toddler and crawling areas should be protected from general walkways and areas used by older children.

- The toilet and hand-washing facilities should be accessible to all indoor and outdoor play areas used by children. When young children need to use the toilet, their need is generally very immediate, and a delay in getting to the facility could mean an "accident." Also, if first aid is required, rapid access to running water is essential.

- Toilets should be located in rooms separate from those used for cooking or eating.

A Room of Their Own

Commercial child-care facilities should have a separate room or designated area for the temporary or ongoing care of a child who needs to be separated from the group due to injury or illness. Locate this space so the child may be supervised and lavatory facilities are readily accessible.

Children who are injured or ill generally need to be separated from other children to allow them to rest and minimize the potential spread of infectious diseases. Even though your policy may be to not provide care to sick children, you still need to be prepared to deal with a child who becomes ill while in your care. If you suspect the child has a communicable disease, clean and disinfect all equipment used by the child.

When not needed for the separation and care of a particular child, this area may be used for other purposes.

- Separate, private toilet facilities should be provided for male and female children six years of age or older. Once independent toilet behavior is established, children should be allowed the opportunity to practice modesty.
- Toilets and sinks should be adequate in number and easily accessible for both use and supervision. Your state will have its own specific requirements, but the following standards can be used for basic planning guidelines. Maximum toilet height should be 11 inches, and maximum sink height should be 22 inches. Have a minimum of one sink and one flush toilet for 10 or fewer toddlers and preschool-age children using toilets; a minimum of one sink and one flush toilet for 15 or fewer school-age children using toilets; a minimum of two sinks and two flush toilets for 16 to 30 children using toilets; and a minimum of one sink and one flush toilet for each additional 15 children. Urinals should not exceed 30 percent of the total required toilet fixtures.

Buy, Don't Rent

If you're going to start in a commercial location, you may assume the best thing to do is to rent a facility. Children's Discovery Centers owner Lois Mitten Rosenberry suggests a different approach: If at all possible, purchase the facility your center is in.

Mitten Rosenberry personally owns all the buildings her centers are in and leases that property to her company. The woman who started her business when her older daughter was on a free-school-lunch program now owns more than $3 million worth of real estate that will be paid for long before she's ready to retire.

"When you rent, you're paying money so the developer or landlord will have the money to make his own payments. At the end of ten years, you have nothing, and the person who owns the real estate has some valuable income-generating property," Mitten Rosenberry observes. "If you can get the down payment and qualify for a mortgage, you'll find your payments probably won't cost you any more than rent, and you're building equity."

If the idea of owning property is a little scary, Mitten Rosenberry thinks you should be more frightened of a lease. If you own the property and things aren't going well, you can sell it; if you sign a lease, you probably won't be able to get out of it. Also, if you own the real estate, you're not at risk of hefty rent increases after you've improved the property and built a successful business.

Mitten Rosenberry says she makes more money from owning and leasing back the property than she takes in salary, which gives her a tax break along with financial security. "If I didn't own the real estate," she says, "I would not be where I am today."

- Toilet-training equipment should be provided for children being toilet-trained. Child-sized toilets or safe, cleanable step aids and modified toilet seats (where adult-sized toilets are present) should be used; potty chairs are not recommended due to the challenges of sanitary handling.

- Toilet rooms should have a door that can be easily opened by children from the inside and barriers that prevent unattended toddler entry. They should also have at least one waste receptacle with a pedal-operated lid.

Beware!

Environmental hazards such as pits, abandoned wells, and abandoned appliances present a risk for entrapment and even burial. Children can fall into wells, pits, and other excavations and can become trapped in refrigerators. These hazards should be remedied or simply made inaccessible to children. Discarded appliances should have their doors removed.

- Hand-washing sinks should be adjacent to diaper changing tables; have at least one sink for every two changing tables.

- Diaper changing tables should have impervious, nonabsorbent surfaces. They should be sturdy, equipped with railings, and of an adult height. They should never be located in food preparation areas. Do not use safety straps; they are difficult to clean and may harbor contaminants and decrease staff-child interaction.

- Provide conveniently located, washable, plastic-lined, tightly covered receptacles that can be operated by a foot pedal for soiled burping cloths and linens.

- Water heating equipment should be capable of heating water to at least 120° F. Where a dishwasher is used, water should be heated to at least 140° F. Install scald-prevention devices on all faucets that are accessible to children.

- Drinking water, dispensed by either fountains or by single-service cups, should be accessible to children while indoors and outdoors. Drinking fountains should have an orifice guard above the rim of the fountain, and pressure should be regulated so the water stream does not contact the orifice guard or splash on the floor, but should rise at least two inches above the orifice guard.

- Play, dining, and napping may be done in the same room (exclusive of bathrooms, kitchens, hallways, and closets), provided that the room is of sufficient size to have a defined area for each of the activities at the time when the activity is underway, the room meets other building requirements, and the use of the room for one purpose does not interfere with use for other purposes. However, infants and toddlers younger than age 2 should be cared for in separate rooms.

- You should have a crib, cot, sleeping bag, bed, mat, or pad for each child who spends more than four hours a day at your facility. To ensure sanitation, comfort, and adequate temperature, when in use these items should be placed at least 3 feet apart, unless separated by screens. Pads should be enclosed in washable covers, used only over carpeting, and long enough so the child's head or feet do not extend off the pad.

- Do not use stacked cribs; the lower cribs can be contaminated with bodily fluids from the upper cribs.

- Provide a separate storage area for each child's and staff member's personal effects and clothing. Each child's property should be labeled with his or her name. Space coat hooks so coats will not touch each other, or provide an appropriately sized individual cubicle or locker for storage.

- Have designated spaces for storage of play and teaching equipment, supplies, and other materials. This enhances safety and provides a good example of an orderly environment.

- Provide facilities for separate storage of soiled and clean linens.

- If you will be caring for school-age children after school, provide a separate area away from the younger children for doing homework. Furnish this area with the appropriate number of tables or desks and chairs. It should be adequately ventilated and properly lighted.

Playground and Outdoor Areas

Children need to play outside—both for their own health and development, and for the sanity of their caregivers. Ideally, your center should be equipped with an outdoor play area that directly adjoins the indoor facilities, or that can be reached by a safe route and is no further than one-eighth of a mile away. You'll need a minimum of 75 square feet for each child using the playground at any one time, and your total outdoor play area should be able to accommodate at least 33 percent of your licensed capacity at one time. While it is good to exceed the minimum requirements of space if possible, do not create such a large recreation area that your staff cannot easily keep watch over the children. Staggered scheduling can be used so that all the children have an opportunity to be outside over a two- or three-hour time period. Every young child should engage in gross motor play at least once (and preferably twice) a day.

The playground should be free of hazards and at least 30 feet away from electrical transformers, high-voltage power lines, electrical substations, air conditioner units, railroad tracks, unenclosed swimming and wading pools, ditches, ponds or other bodies of water, or sources of toxic fumes or gases. Fencing or another state-approved form of barrier should surround the play area, and any twist wires, bolts, or other sharp edges on fencing material should be on the side away from the playground. The barrier should be at least 4 feet high, with a bottom edge that is no more than 3.5 inches above the ground. The barrier should be constructed to discourage climbing and have openings no greater than 3.5 inches to prevent both entrapment and climbing.

Beware!

Most children who drown do so within a few feet of safety and in the presence of a supervising adult. Swimming and wading pools and other water hazards should be enclosed with a fence that is at least 5 feet high and comes to within 3.5 inches of the ground. Gates should be constructed to discourage climbing, with self-closing, positive-latching gates; install locking devices at least 55 inches from the ground.

An outdoor playground should have at least two exits, with one remote from the buildings. Equip gates with self-closing and positive self-latching mechanisms, attached high enough so the gate cannot be opened by a small child.

A rooftop may be used as a play area as long as it is enclosed with a fence at least 6 feet high and designed to prevent children from climbing it. You must have an approved fire escape leading from the roof to an open space at the ground level that meets the safety standards for outdoor play areas.

Arrange the outdoor play area so that it is completely visible to staff at all times to avoid injury and abuse. Provide ample space for the use of each playground item—generally, 9 feet around fixed items and 15 feet around any moving part. Be sure the space allocated to one piece of equipment does not encroach on that of another piece of equipment. In addition, all fixed play equipment should have a minimum of 9 feet clearance from walkways, hard surfaces, buildings, and other structures that are not part of play activities.

Provide storage space—either indoors or outdoors—for any playground equipment not secured to the ground.

You also need a mix of sunlit and shaded areas. While most children benefit from time in the sun (unless a medical condition dictates otherwise), they also need to be protected from excessive exposure.

Outdoor paved surfaces should be designed to drain well to avoid water accumulation and ice formation, and all walking surfaces should have a nonslip finish and be free of holes and any irregularities in the surface.

Walkways, Stairs, and Railings

Your center should have safe, clearly marked pickup and drop-off points, and established procedures for their use.

Identify all safe pedestrian crosswalks and bike routes in the vicinity of your facility, include them in your safety plan (in case an evacuation is ever necessary), and communicate that information to all children, parents, and staff.

All inside and outside stairs, ramps, porches, and walkways should be safe, well-lighted, and constructed according to local building codes.

For centers serving preschoolers and school-age children, porches, landings, balconies, stairs, and similar structures should have bottom guardrails no more than 2 feet above the floor. For centers serving infants and toddlers, bottom guardrails should be no more than 6 inches above the floor. Protective handrails and guardrails should have supports placed at intervals of less than 3.5 inches or should be equipped with sufficient protective material to prevent a 3.5-inch sphere from passing between the rails.

On all stairways consisting of three or more steps, handrails at children's height should be installed on both sides of the stairway and be securely attached to either the walls or stairs. Place securely installed, effective gates at the top and bottom of each open stairway. Separate basement stairways by a full door at the main-floor level; this door should be self-closing and kept locked when the basement is not in use.

Health, Safety, and Sanitation Practices

Whether you run a commercial center or a family child-care center, you must follow certain health, safety, and sanitation practices. Understanding these practices will help you make good decisions in the design and setup of your center.

- Hand-washing sinks should never be used for rinsing soiled clothing or for cleaning toilet-training equipment. Be sure separate sinks are conveniently located for these tasks.

- Centers with more than 30 children should have a mop sink that is used only for such purposes.

- Diaper changing tables should never be used for temporary placement or serving of food.

- When children are resting, pads and sleeping bags should not be placed directly on concrete, linoleum, hardwood, or tile floors.

- Store sleeping mats so there is no contact with the sleeping surface of another mat. This helps prevent the transmission of such diseases as lice, scabies, and ringworm.

- Closet doors that are accessible to children should have an inside release so the door can be opened by a child inside the closet to prevent entrapment.

Beware!

Health, safety, and sanitation are serious issues in a child-care center. If a child is injured or becomes ill due to your negligence in these areas, you'll not only have to deal with your own feelings of guilt and responsibility, but you'll also likely face litigation, possible civil and criminal liability, and negative publicity that could put you out of business.

- Matches and lighters should always be kept in a place inaccessible to children.
- Regardless of their intended use, store thin plastic bags, including trash can liners, out of reach of children.
- Strings and cords long enough to encircle a child's neck (6 inches or more) should not be accessible to children. Unintentional strangulation deaths of children have been caused by such items as pacifier cords, highchair straps, and window-covering cords, usually during play.
- When arranging outdoor playground equipment, metal items, especially slides, should be placed in the shade when possible or at least oriented in a north-south direction to reduce buildup of heat in the metal.
- The soil in play areas should not contain hazardous levels of any toxic chemical or substance. If you have reason to believe a problem may exist, have the soil tested by your local health department, extension service, or an environmental control testing laboratory.

Setting Up a Homebased Center

If you've decided to open a child-care center at home, discuss your plans with family members and your neighbors before you open. Younger children may resent other children coming into your home and changing their lifestyle. Older children—especially teenagers—will need to be told what's expected of them and what they can expect as your business gets off the ground. Spouses may not completely understand the time commitment involved in this business, so talk about things in detail well in advance of bringing the first client in. You may find that your extended family and friends do not comprehend what's involved in a professional child-care business and may take the attitude that since you're at home during the day, you're "not really working" or you're "just baby-sitting."

Talk to your neighbors about the impact your business will have on them in terms of traffic (as parents drop off and pick up their children) and noise (think about the decibel levels five or six children can generate when playing). Let them know what steps you'll take to keep any irritation or inconvenience to a minimum, and reassure them that they should feel free to contact you with any concerns or questions.

Operating a family child-care center means sacrificing a certain amount of your own personal privacy. "Your home becomes a public place, and that can be a problem," Exeter, California, child-care provider Janet Hale says. "You have people coming and going all the time—the kids, their parents, the licensing people."

At the same time, always remember that this is your home and you set the rules—and those rules may be different than what the children have to follow at home. "When in my home, the children are expected to follow my house rules," says Suzanne

Wright. "The parents understand that I am still in control until the child has been taken out of my house."

Some family child-care center operators have certain rooms of their homes designated for their business; others use their entire homes. Your decision will be based on your state guidelines and personal preferences. Wright uses the main level of her house for the children's play area, with sleeping space upstairs; the basement is off-limits for safety reasons. Christine Srabian has a sunroom that serves as her primary child-care area, but she allows the children to go into other parts of the house, depending on their age and the activity they are participating in.

Childproofing Your Home

Go through every room of your home and check for potential health and safety hazards. Even rooms you intend to be off-limits to the children you care for should be childproofed.

All unused electrical outlets should be covered. Cleaning supplies, medicines, and other potentially dangerous chemicals should be stored on high shelves or in locked cabinets. All lower cabinets in your kitchen should have childproof latches. Sharp and breakable objects should be placed out of reach of curious little hands. Block stairs with gates. Install locks on doors high enough so children can't reach them and use doorknob covers to help prevent children from entering rooms with possible dangers. Use window guards and safety netting to help prevent falls from windows, balconies, decks, and landings.

Corner and edge bumpers can help prevent injuries from falls against sharp edges of furniture and fireplaces. Doorstops and door holders can help prevent small fingers and hands from being pinched or crushed in doors.

Have a fire extinguisher in your kitchen and smoke detectors on every floor. Depending on the layout of your house, you may want more than one smoke detector per floor. Check this equipment monthly to make sure it's working.

Use anti-scald devices for faucets and shower heads, and set your water heater temperature to 120 degrees to help prevent burns from hot water.

Smart Tip _Tip..._

If you're starting a family child-care business and you have children, be sure to set appropriate boundaries so their privacy and belongings are respected.

▲

If you own any firearms, pellet or BB guns, or dart or cap pistols, they should be unloaded and kept under lock and key in areas inaccessible to the children.

Pets

Many child-care providers who care for children in their own homes have pets. Pets can be excellent companions for children. They can meet some of the emotional needs of children and others. Caring for pets also gives children an opportunity to learn how to treat and be responsible for others. However, some guidelines for protecting the health and safety of the children should be followed.

- All pets, whether kept indoors or outside, should be in good health, show no evidence of disease, and be friendly toward children.
- Dogs or cats should be appropriately immunized (check with your veterinarian) and be kept on flea, tick, and worm control programs. Proof of immunizations should be kept in a safe place.
- Pet living quarters should be kept clean. All pet waste should be disposed of immediately. Litter boxes should not be accessible to children.
- Child-care providers should always be present when children play with pets.
- Children should be taught how to behave around a pet. They should be taught not to provoke the pet or remove the pet's food. They should always keep their faces away from a pet's mouth, beak, or claws.
- If you have a pet in your child-care facility, tell parents before they enroll their child. Some children have allergies that may require the parents to find other child-care arrangements.
- Children should wash their hands after handling pets or pet items.
- Keep in mind that all reptiles can potentially carry salmonella. Therefore, small reptiles that might be handled by children, including turtles and iguanas, can easily transmit salmonella to them. Therefore, iguanas and turtles are not appropriate pets for child-care centers.
- Some pets, particularly "exotic" pets such as some turtles, iguanas, venomous or aggressive snakes, spiders, and tropical fish may not be appropriate in the child-care setting. Check with a veterinarian if you are unsure whether a particular pet is appropriate for children. Contact your local health department for regulations and advice regarding pets in the child-care setting.

If you have pets, you may use them to help the children learn to treat animals properly and with respect, or you may keep them totally separate from the kids—the choice is yours.

7

Furnishing and Equipping Your Center

Many child-care centers try to create an ambience that is both fun and educational, using colors, figures, shapes, and other elements to create a playful, imaginative environment where children will feel comfortable. As you work on your décor, keep in mind that your primary goal is to appeal to children. For the most part, you'll want to keep furnishings and fixtures on a scale appropriate to children who are less than three feet tall.

Keep in mind that a group of children—even a small group—can make quite a mess, particularly on floors. Take advantage of the fact that multiple textures are fascinating to children, so include both tile or vinyl flooring and heavy-duty, stain-resistant carpeting. Use the tile or vinyl in areas where paint will be used and food will be eaten for easier cleanup.

You will also want to consider noise issues—children are loud. You can take several design steps to minimize noise, both for your staff's sanity and to prevent one class or activity group's loud play from disturbing another's quieter activity. On the floor, carpeting is better for noise insulation than tile or other hard surfaces. Acoustic tiles on the ceiling will help absorb noise. Look for ways to increase the sound-absorption quality of walls. One very affordable treatment is to cover walls with cork, then with a durable, colorful fabric; in doing this, you've created wall-to-wall bulletin boards that will not only reduce noise but provide a place to display projects and artwork.

Large rooms tend to work best in a child-care center. Proper arrangement of furniture and shelving can define various play and activity areas. Windows are also important; children tend to become restless when they feel closed-in, whether it's because they're in a tiny room or because of a lack of windows allowing them to see outdoors.

Specific Rooms

In a commercial child-care center, you will have a number of different rooms with different purposes to consider furnishing and equipping. In addition to the rooms discussed below, you'll also want to consider a kitchen and laundry facilities, which are addressed in Chapter 8.

Lobby/Reception Area

Your lobby needs to be functional but not large. Allow just enough space to accommodate a small reception desk and six or eight chairs for parents and children to use when waiting for each other. The desk and chairs should be low enough to be useful and nonintimidating to children, but high enough to serve your receptionist and the parents who will also be using them.

Go for a lighthearted, casual atmosphere that blends with the overall décor of your center. Pastel colors, lots of light, and youthful decorations—

> ### Bright Idea
>
> Let the children provide your décor. Janet Hale uses gingerbread as her background theme but uses the children's art for the primary décor. She says, "Children should [be exposed to] lots of color and lots of stimulation, and their art should be shown off because it promotes self-esteem."

perhaps some made by the children themselves—will set a good tone. Dark, heavy furniture and somber decorations will not create an atmosphere that is comfortable and attractive for children.

Office

You'll need a small, simply furnished office to do administrative work, make phone calls, and have private conversations with staff members and parents who are considering your center or who have children in your care. Ideally, it should be near or directly adjacent to the lobby. The décor should be neat and attractive, but not lavish. A desk, chairs, a filing cabinet, and perhaps some bookshelves will be sufficient furnishings. The actual equipment you'll need is discussed in Chapter 9.

Classrooms

You will need a classroom for every age group you intend to serve. Classrooms should be large and arranged to create different play or activity areas. There should be a considerable amount of open floor space in the middle of the room to allow children to move about freely, play indoor games, form a circle for storytelling and show-and-tell activities, and to give them a place to sleep with blankets and floor mats during nap time.

Each classroom should have access to outdoor play areas and the lobby without having to disturb other classes. Access may be direct or through a corridor.

As you plan your classrooms, keep your state's required square footage-per-child ratio in mind. More space taken up in the classroom with such installations as cabinets and closets means fewer children can be admitted, so clever use of wall space can be critical. Store items to which children do not need direct access in cabinets or on shelves high off the floor rather than in cases that sit on the ground and take up valuable floor space. Closets should be built with shelving inside. If closets don't extend to the ceiling, use the tops for additional storage, such as for sleeping mats.

Most of your storage for items that will be used for the children's care should be accomplished within the classrooms. Of course, items related to laundry and kitchen activities should be stored in those areas. Plan your space efficiently to maximize its usage under your state laws.

Each child should have his or her own space to store personal belongings. A cubbyhole, such as a wall-mounted box roughly 18 to 24 square inches, works well for this. In

Recommended Classroom Furnishings

This list provides recommended basic items for a large child-care center serving up to 160 youngsters throughout the day:

❑ 75 classroom stacking chairs

❑ 6 round tables

❑ 12 rectangular tables

❑ 160 to 180 floor mats, covers, pillows, and blankets

❑ 8 storage cabinets (for toys and educational materials)

❑ 160 to 180 cubbyholes and coat hooks for children's personal belongings

addition, each child should have a peg from which to hang a jacket. The pegs and cubbyholes should be no more than 3 feet above the floor and should include a place where they can be clearly labeled with the child's name.

When purchasing classroom furniture, consider the size of the children who will be using it. Stacking chairs should be sturdy and low to the ground. Quality polypropylene and steel stacking chairs of a height appropriate for preschoolers can be purchased for $30 to $60 each, depending on brand, with the possibility of quantity discounts. Consider the height of the tables as well. Generally, a good table height for a preschool classroom is 24 inches. Expect to spend $100 to $175 each for either round or rectangular tables.

You'll also need floor mats, pillows, and blankets for nap times. Floor mats will provide a level of comfort similar to cots, and are easier to set up and store. They should have a durable canvas exterior to withstand the rigors of everyday use. Mats that fold into halves or thirds are easier to store than those that don't fold. You'll pay $13 to $25 per mat. You should also purchase an equal number of bed coverings that will fit snugly around the mats, plus pillows and blankets. Alternatively, you could have parents be responsible for providing clean pillows and linens for their children.

For storage, large 72-inch locking steel cabinets will be sufficient. Although you could easily spend much more, you can get basic cabinets for $175 to $225 each at office supply stores.

Choosing the Right Toys

The most visible type of equipment in your child-care center will be toys. Of course, toys should be fun—but they also need to promote learning and development, and above all, they should be safe for the youngsters who are going to be playing with them.

"We look for toys that promote individual play and learning," says Gingerbread House owner Janet Hale. "We have playhouses, dolls, and those kinds of things because they promote nurturing. We don't have a lot of mechanized toys. Most of our toys require interaction for the children to play with."

"I have toys to provide interest and learning," says Suzanne Wright. "Infants enjoy mobiles that they can lie beneath and touch as they get older. They also enjoy 'stations' that provide music and movement when kicked or grabbed from a lying position. Once they can hold objects, small rattles are great. For one- to three-year-olds, I find that large interlocking blocks, shape sorters, push toys such as cars or buses, hard-paged books, and an erasable drawing pad all keep them interested. And telephones are a must!" She observes that at about age 3, boys' and girls' interests begin to differ. Boys generally gravitate toward action figures and cars; most girls enjoy playing with dolls. "Dress-up clothes are always a hit with all kids, as are pretend food and dishes," she says.

Small toys and toy parts available to infants and toddlers should meet the federal small parts standards for toys. The elimination of small parts from children's environment will greatly reduce the risk of injury and fatality due to choking on small parts. Toys or objects that have diameters of less than 1 inch, objects with removable parts that have diameters of less than 1 inch, toys with sharp points and edges, plastic bags and Styrofoam objects should not be accessible to children under four years of age. Often, toys that do not meet the small parts standard are sometimes labeled "intended for children ages three and up." But choking on small parts occurs throughout the preschool years, so it is prudent to keep small parts away from children at least up to age four. Also, children have been known to choke on toys or toy parts that meet federal standards, so you must be vigilant.

The federal standard that applies to toys and other articles intended for use by children under age three is in the Code of Federal Regulations, Title 16, Part 1501, which may be available in your local library; or you can find it online at www.gpoaccess.gov, or order it from the U.S. Government Printing Office (see Appendix). A number of items are exempt from this standard but still could be a choking hazard and should be kept away from children under age four. Those items include coins, rubber balloons, safety pins, and marbles. Practically speaking, objects available to children under age four should not be small enough to fit entirely into a child's mouth.

Toilet-Training Equipment

Potty chairs are difficult to keep clean and out of reach of children. Small-size flushable toilets or modified toilet seats and step aids are preferable. If potty chairs are used for toilet-training, you should use them only in a bathroom area and out of reach of toilets or other potty chairs. After each use of a potty chair, you should:

- Immediately empty the contents into a toilet, being careful not to splash or touch the water in the toilet.
- Rinse the potty with water from a sink used only for custodial cleaning. Do not rinse the potty in a sink used for washing hands. A sink used for food preparation should never be used for rinsing a potty chair.
- Dump the rinse water into a toilet.
- Wash and disinfect the potty chair.
- Wash and disinfect the sink and all exposed surfaces.
- Wash your hands thoroughly.

Playground Equipment

Six factors will govern the selection of your playground equipment:

1. The size of the outdoor play area

2. The age of the children who will be using the playground

3. The number of children who will be using the playground at any given time

4. Safety issues

5. Insurance considerations

6. Cost

As much as children love to climb on monkey bars and play on slides and swings, you should reserve the majority of your play area as open space where they can simply run around and expend excess energy, as well as play outdoor games. Do not cover more than 30 to 40 percent of the ground with unmovable equipment.

All outdoor play equipment should be of safe design, in good repair, and made to match the body dimensions of children. Install equipment so an average adult cannot cause a fixed structure to wobble or tip. Moving parts (such as swing components, teeter-totter mechanisms, spring ride springs, etc.) should be shielded or enclosed to prevent pinching, catching, or crushing of body parts or catching of scarves, mittens, hood strings, etc. Check to make sure all pieces of equipment are free of sharp edges and protruding parts. Sand wood materials until smooth and inspect them regularly for splintering.

Tailoring the equipment for age is important for both safety and fun. A 20-foot-tall slide may

> **Tip...**
>
> **Smart Tip**
> Limit access to play equipment according to the age groups for which the equipment is developmentally appropriate. This will reduce the risk of injury and provide a proper play experience.

Recommended Playground Equipment

A possible, but not definitive, list of playground equipment for a child-care center serving 75 to 125 children a day might include:

❏ 1 set of state-approved swings (to be used by children three years old and up)

❏ 1 or 2 slides

❏ 1 or 2 sets of monkey bars

❏ 4 to 8 vinyl or rubber balls

❏ 1 basic gym unit with base pads

❏ 2 or 3 4-foot-tall basketball goals

look impressive and exciting on your playground, but most three-year-olds will find it intimidating, not to mention that it's a serious safety risk. The maximum height of playground equipment used by children up to age three is 3 feet, and 5.5 feet if children between the ages of three and six have access to it.

Surround all pieces of the playground equipment with a resilient surface, such as fine, loose sand, wood chips, or wood mulch at least 9 inches deep. Rubber mats manufactured for such use are an acceptable alternative. The resilient surface should extend at least 4 feet beyond the fall zone of the equipment. If you use particulate resilient material, check it at least once a month for packing due to rain or ice. If it is compressed, turn it over or rake it up to restore its resilience.

Sandboxes should be constructed to permit drainage. Cover them tightly and securely when not in use, and be sure they are kept free from cat or other animal excrement. Do not allow children to dig or play in sand used under swings and as a resilient surface around other equipment. It is not necessary to cover sand used this way, and therefore, such sand could contain contaminants from animals or insects.

Dollar Stretcher

Shop for equipment at trade shows, where exhibitors have their latest items on display but may not want to pack them up and take them home. Go with a truck and be prepared to haul the items away yourself. You can get some great prices on brand-new items.

If you have room, a few tricycles can provide considerable entertainment for toddlers and preschoolers. However, there must be enough open space for youngsters to use them without risking a collision with other riders or children.

A low-cost playground toy is a simple rubber ball that can be kicked or thrown. A soft, large, round rubber ball is better than a relatively hard ball, such as a soccer ball. The ball shouldn't be hard enough to hurt or bruise a child who accidentally gets hit. Beach balls are a good idea and can provide plenty of safe fun, but they aren't especially durable and will easily fly away on a windy day.

Toddler versions of sporting equipment are popular and inexpensive. Basketball hoops that stand 4 or 5 feet tall are perfect for young children who have a few years to go before they can qualify for the NBA. Child-sized footballs, which are softer and smaller than regulation footballs, and baseball equipment (foam or plastic bats that won't hurt if thrown or used to hit another person) can be useful as well, particularly if you intend to incorporate organized outdoor games into your lessons. If your balls and related toys are made of spongy foam rubber, be sure to store them indoors and don't use them when the play area is wet or covered in snow. A fair selection of several kinds of balls and related equipment will cost $100 to $150.

The number of children using the play area will strongly influence the quantity of your equipment. For example, a slide and climbing complex that can only accommodate three or four youngsters at a time will be sufficient if you'll have fewer than 15 or 20 kids using the area at one time. But if you'll have 30 children on the playground at once, you will need more of everything—slides, swings, jungle gyms, balls, etc.

Safety, of course, must be a consideration. Most children's toys and playground equipment will come with a manufacturer's recommendation for appropriate ages. Start with that label, and consider how the toy will be used at your facility and how much

> **Tip...**
>
> **Smart Tip**
>
> Many equipment manu-facturers will consult with you, usually at no charge, on the best way to set up your playground. You may want to consider how helpful a manu-facturer is with this process when choosing which one(s) to buy from.

Something Old, Something New

Should you buy new or used when furnishing and equipping your center? Certainly used equipment and toys will save you money at first, but they may not last long. You'll also need to consider liability issues; manufacturers may not accept responsibility for equipment not purchased directly from them or an authorized dealer, and/or not installed by an approved source.

Then there's the image issue. Lois Mitten Rosenberry says she always buys new because that is consistent with the high-quality image she wants to project. Also, she says, new equipment will generally stand up to intense wear and tear better than used equipment. She says, "That doesn't mean if I'm at a garage sale and I see something that looks brand new that I wouldn't buy it, because I have."

supervision it will require. On slides and climbing structures, look at safety rails and consider how difficult the steps will be for a toddler to manage. Avoid products with a wide age range. For example, a jungle gym intended for children from age 3 to 15 may be too challenging for many youngsters on the lower end of the spectrum—and not challenging enough for the older ones.

ASTM International (see Appendix) publishes several references for playground equipment, including Standard Consumer Safety Performance Specification for Playground Equipment for Public Use (F1487-98) and Standard Consumer Safety Performance Specification for Home Playground Equipment (F1148-98c).

Maintain a file of all information and records pertaining to the manufacturing, installation, and regular inspection of the playground equipment.

Audiovisual and Computer Equipment

You may want to include audiovisual and computer instruction in your program of activities.

The basics in audiovisual equipment are a television and a DVD player. If you have a stock of videos, you may also want a VCR, but most movies and other programs are available on DVD now. The key consideration in purchasing a television is reach. You must decide how large an audience (10 children? 50 children?) will be watching at any given time and choose a television of sufficient screen size and speaker volume to be clearly visible and audible. A tiny, poor-quality television will not hold the attention of active young children for long.

The DVD player doesn't need to be anything special; the average model will meet your needs. You don't need to make the extravagant expense of equipping every room with its own audio-video center, particularly since such passive activities are not likely to comprise a significant portion of the children's day. Having one or two mobile sets will allow you to bring out the equipment (for example, on rainy days when you can't send the children outside for playtime) to whichever class needs it at the moment. A sturdy metal cart with wheels will do the job nicely.

Expect to spend anywhere from $200 to $800 on a television and another $100 to $200 on a DVD player.

Inventory

A child-care center is not an inventory business; however, you will need to maintain quantities of classrooms supplies; diapers for changing infants; cleaning supplies; laundry, food, and beverage supplies; and office supplies. See Chapter 8 for more on laundry, food, and beverage issues and Chapter 9 for details on office supplies.

Classroom Supplies

You will need scores of supplies to keep children active and busy during the day. Remember that you will be seeing most of these children for eight or ten hours a day, five days a week, for months or years. Then consider the attention span of the average four-year-old. It should be obvious that you're going to need the supplies and equipment necessary to facilitate a wide range of stimulating activities.

Art supplies can be a considerable classroom expense. Exactly which supplies you need depends on the activities you intend to schedule, and the quantities depend on the frequency of the activities and the number of children participating.

A basic stock of art supplies should include crayons, colored markers, paints, brushes, butcher paper (for painting), bond paper (for crayon and marker drawing), safety scissors, colored construction paper, coloring books, puzzles and games (geared, of course, to the ages of the children you serve), tape, glue, and paste.

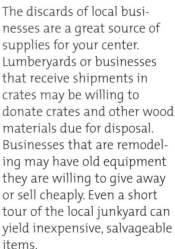

Dollar Stretcher

The discards of local businesses are a great source of supplies for your center. Lumberyards or businesses that receive shipments in crates may be willing to donate crates and other wood materials due for disposal. Businesses that are remodeling may have old equipment they are willing to give away or sell cheaply. Even a short tour of the local junkyard can yield inexpensive, salvageable items.

When selecting crayons, markers, and paints, consider color, variety, and toxicity. Most children's art supplies can be found in nontoxic varieties that will not cause any harm if misused. Also, water-soluble markers and paints will be popular with the parents, who have to wash (and buy) the children's clothes.

Because you will need a considerable supply of most of these items, try to buy in bulk. Wholesale art suppliers and warehouse-style stores are good sources.

Cleaning Supplies

Though you may limit your child-care center to children who are toilet-trained, there will still be accidents. Of course, you may care for children in diapers as well, which means you will need supplies for changing babies and toddlers. Though you may require parents to provide a supply of diapers for their child, you should have some on hand for emergencies. You will also need to stock rubber or plastic gloves, and wipes for cleaning the children.

Further, you will need standard cleaning supplies, including glass cleaner, all-purpose kitchen and bathroom cleaners, air fresheners, and disinfectants. You should have a regular schedule for cleaning and disinfecting the classroom area and toys to maintain a healthy environment. This schedule should be accelerated during cold and flu seasons.

Consider how you'll dispose of soiled diapers. Odor-reducing bags or bags that seal air-tight will be needed for the sanitary disposal of soiled diapers and wipes. See Chapter 14 for more on keeping your facility clean and sanitary.

Health and Safety Standards

A knowledge of certain health and safety standards will help you make good decisions about equipping your facility and maintaining the proper items in inventory.

Be sure all the arts and crafts materials used in your facility are nontoxic. To prevent contamination and injury, do not allow any eating or drinking by children or staff during the use of such materials.

Be sure all poisonous or potentially harmful plants on the premises are inaccessible to children. All plants that are accessible to children should be identified and verified as safe with your local poison control center. Remember, plants are among the most common household substances ingested by children, and it's difficult to determine every commercially available household plant's toxicity. The safest and most reasonable approach is to simply keep indoor plants out of the reach of children, choose your exterior landscaping with care, and watch children carefully when they are outdoors to make sure they do not ingest any parts of an outside plant.

Do not use carpets made of nylon, Orlon, wood and/or silk, or other materials that emit highly toxic fumes when they burn; to do so would risk poisoning even during an evacuation.

Test any surface painted before 1978 for excessive lead levels. Lead is prohibited in contemporary paints, but if there is any doubt about the presence of lead in the existing paint, contact your local health department for information regarding testing.

Recommended First-Aid Supplies

Keep a fully stocked first-aid kit within easy reach of all caregivers but out of reach of children. Check your kit(s) regularly, and restock as necessary. Your first-aid kit should include:

- ❏ Box of nonporous disposable gloves
- ❏ Sealed packages of alcohol wipes or antiseptic
- ❏ Small scissors
- ❏ Cold pack
- ❏ Tweezers (for removing splinters)
- ❏ Thermometer
- ❏ Adhesive bandage tape
- ❏ Sterile gauze squares (2 inches and 3 inches)
- ❏ Triangular bandages
- ❏ Flexible roller gauze (1-inch and 2-inch widths)
- ❏ Triangular bandages
- ❏ Safety pins
- ❏ Eye dressing
- ❏ Insect-sting preparation
- ❏ Pencil and notepad
- ❏ Syrup of ipecac
- ❏ Small splints
- ❏ Sealable plastic bags for soiled materials

Kitchen and Laundry Facilities

Though you may not be required by law to have kitchen and laundry facilities on the premises of your child-care center (remember, state laws vary), these amenities allow you to provide a higher level of service and care. For most family child-care facilities, your home's kitchen and laundry equipment should be adequate, although state regulations may require you to make some modifications. This chapter focuses on equipment for a commercial center, although the food-handling, nutrition, and behavioral information apply to any size child-care operation.

Kitchen

Having a fully equipped kitchen in your child-care center means that you can serve hot meals and have a place to store snacks, drinks, and other food-related supplies. The kitchen doesn't have to be elaborate but should contain basic food preparation equipment and adhere to legal and health department requirements for food-service operations.

Expect the kitchen to take up about 15 to 20 percent of your total space. Within this area, you will have space for receiving, storage, food preparation, cooking, cleanup, and trash storage. Most child-care center kitchens are situated toward the rear of the building with easy access from back entryways to make delivery of supplies more efficient. For added convenience, consider installing double doors at the receiving port and have a dolly available for moving heavy and stacked boxes.

A pantry or wall shelves for dry storage and a large refrigerator/freezer for storing perishable goods, juices, milk, and ice should be located immediately adjacent to the receiving area. You'll need either plenty of counter space for food preparation or a dedicated food preparation table.

Although equipment needs vary, most child-care centers serving hot lunches (or breakfasts or suppers, if you decide to operate during nontraditional hours) will have to equip a preparation kitchen. The basic equipment you will need include a toaster, microwave oven, convection oven, utensil rack, mixer, slicer, food cutter, blender, griddle top range with oven, broiler, and a refrigerator and freezer. A good fryer is optional. Budget between $27,000 and $40,000 for your major production equipment. Figure on spending another $1,000 to $2,500 for small items such as ladles, tongs, spoons, pans, potholders, spatulas, and can openers.

The dishwashing and trash areas should be positioned toward the rear of the kitchen away from food production. Set up the dishwashing area with at least a two-compartment sink with a side area where dishes can be placed in racks after they are rinsed before being placed in the dishwasher.

A small, three-stage dishwashing machine made by a major manufacturer will cost $3,000

> **Beware!**
> Maintain at least 18 inches of space between a drinking fountain and any sink or towel dispenser. This helps prevent contamination of the fountain by organisms being splashed or deposited during handwashing.

Recommended Kitchen Equipment

The following equipment list would be appropriate for a kitchen in a child-care center serving more than 160 children:

- ❏ 1 stove, oven and range
- ❏ 2 refrigerators, 16 cubic feet each
- ❏ 1 freezer, 20 cubic feet
- ❏ 1 commercial dishwasher
- ❏ 1 electric hand mixer
- ❏ 1 toaster
- ❏ 1 microwave oven
- ❏ 1 utensil rack
- ❏ 1 mixer
- ❏ 1 slicer
- ❏ 1 food cutter
- ❏ 1 meat grinder
- ❏ 1 blender
- ❏ 1 broiler
- ❏ 1 three-compartment sink
- ❏ 160 to 180 plates
- ❏ 50 to 60 bowls
- ❏ 100 tumblers
- ❏ 2 to 4 serving platters
- ❏ 12 divided serving bowls
- ❏ 6 pitchers
- ❏ 2 to 6 serving spoons
- ❏ 2 commercial-size saucepans
- ❏ 1 12-quart double boiler
- ❏ 2 bake and roast pans
- ❏ 10 3-quart plastic containers with lids
- ❏ 2 8-quart plastic containers with lids
- ❏ 1 stainless-steel chef knife
- ❏ 1 stainless-steel serrated bread knife
- ❏ 1 stainless-steel slotted cook's spoon
- ❏ 1 stainless-steel solid cook's spoon
- ❏ 1 stainless-steel French knife
- ❏ 1 stainless-steel cook's fork
- ❏ 1 pair of stainless-steel utility tongs
- ❏ 2 stainless-steel sandwich spreaders
- ❏ 1 tin funnel
- ❏ 1 stainless-steel can punch
- ❏ 2 vegetable peelers
- ❏ 2 rubber spatulas
- ❏ 3 aluminum dredges
- ❏ 1 measuring spoon set
- ❏ 1 aluminum measuring container
- ❏ 24 aluminum muffin tins
- ❏ 24 aluminum cookie sheets
- ❏ 4 syrup dispensers
- ❏ 1 stainless-steel tableware transporter
- ❏ 1 heavy-duty can opener
- ❏ 1 stainless-steel egg beater
- ❏ 50 to 75 stainless-steel table forks
- ❏ 50 to 75 stainless-steel teaspoons
- ❏ 4 serving trays
- ❏ 1 serving cart (optional)

to $9,000. Installing the equipment, complete with landing area, dish table, garbage disposal, and three-compartment sink, will cost anywhere from $4,000 to $20,000.

There are less capital-intensive options as well, such as installing a three-compartment sink and doing all the dishes by hand. If your state regulations allow it and you'd like to give the old-fashioned way a try, figure on spending $1,500 to $2,000 for a sink. Keep in mind, though, that your water temperature may not be hot enough to meet OSHA or local health department standards.

Although price is certainly important, it is not the only factor to consider when choosing your kitchen equipment. You can minimize labor costs by purchasing equipment that is fully automatic and self-cleaning whenever possible. Reduce utility expenses by installing modern, energy-efficient items.

Buying from well-known manufacturers that have reliable equipment and a network of repair facilities is also important. Look for standard lines that are both versatile and mobile so you'll not have to duplicate hardware. Avoid custom-designed lines; standard equipment is generally priced lower from the start and is less expensive to install. It is also going to be less expensive to repair and/or replace when necessary.

Ventilation

Across the country, pollution control is tightening, and new regulations are being introduced every year. This has had a significant impact on ventilation requirements. New, more efficient systems that meet the more stringent requirements have increased the cost of outfitting a kitchen. Expect to pay $150 to $400 per linear foot for a hood and grease filter, and $18 to $48 per linear foot for ductwork. Ventilation systems are expensive to install, but they offer a tremendous opportunity for energy conservation. The more efficient systems are worth their extra cost because they contribute to substantially lower monthly utility bills. Check with prominent heating, ventilation, and air conditioning (HVAC) system manufacturers and installers to find the best options for your particular facility.

You have three basic ventilation system options. The first is reducing the quantity of exhaust air, which will decrease the exhaust fan size and, ultimately, your purchasing and operating costs. In conjunction with this option, you can also reduce the amount of makeup (fresh) air you have to introduce to compensate for the amount of exhaust air you release. This, in turn, will reduce the size of the makeup air fan you need, along with its purchasing and operating cost. Finally, you can change the method of introducing makeup air so that it doesn't need to be conditioned; this will significantly reduce the air-handling cost.

One of the best ways to achieve a reduction in exhaust air and makeup air is to install a high-velocity, low-volume system, which reduces the exhaust air output by 40 percent. This directly affects the makeup air quantities, because makeup and exhaust

Bright Idea

Instead of hiring a cook, consider contracting with a catering company to provide lunches and snacks for the children. You may find it more efficient and reliable than trying to do it yourself, and the overall cost may not be significantly different.

must balance, and results in savings from processing the makeup air. A key benefit of such a system is the introduction of raw, unconditioned air directly to the exhaust ventilator, a process that eliminates the cost of heating or cooling a portion of the makeup air.

Food and Beverage Supplies

Generally, you'll get the best prices on nonperishable foods, such as cereal and oatmeal, when you buy in bulk. For easier storage and lower cost, buy juices in powdered mixes or frozen concentrates, also in bulk quantities.

Perishable foods, such as fruit, milk, and bread, must be bought carefully to prevent waste though spoilage. Thorough menu-planning is an important part of shopping for perishable items.

Nonperishable goods should be stored in cabinets with doors that close snugly and have no cracks or gaps through which insects and vermin might infiltrate. Keep food containers tightly sealed and the kitchen area clean to minimize the attraction of pests. If you notice signs of infestation, take action immediately. Use baited traps rather than spraying insecticide around food. The danger of contaminating food intended for children is even greater than for adults because children have a far lower tolerance for most poisons.

The types of food you need will be based on the meals you serve. School-age children who use your center only in the afternoon will require just a snack. Milk or juice, a piece of fruit, and/or a peanut butter and jelly sandwich will suffice. Children who will be at your center all day will require lunch and a snack (and for younger toddlers, two snacks, depending on your latest pickup time). You can either offer a simple, complete lunch and price your service accordingly, or stipulate that children bring their own lunches, and provide milk and juice for that meal and a snack for the afternoon.

Christine Srabian requires parents to provide all food for infants until they are eating regular table food. "Children all start different foods at different stages," she says. "This one is eating peaches, but that one hasn't tried peaches yet. They need to try foods at home before they eat those items at my house. We don't want any allergic reactions."

Bright Idea

If you run a small or homebased center, occasionally treat the children to takeout food. Consider having pizza delivered one day a week, or arrange for burgers and fries once in a while.

Good Nutrition and Mealtime Behavior

Eating nutritious food and learning good mealtime behavior are important for children due to the rapid growth and the major developmental changes that they undergo. Mealtimes can also be an opportunity for learning and developing social and motor skills, and for being introduced to new kinds of foods. Skills such as hand-washing, table manners, and carrying on a conversation at the table can be developed and reinforced. Age-appropriate motor skills can be fostered by encouraging children to use child-sized utensils and to clear their dishes and utensils from the table. Child-sized furniture and hand-washing sinks help children feel comfortable as well as help them learn.

Make sure that all children and staff wash their hands both before and after eating. Serve food "family style" and eat as a group. This gives the provider the opportunity to promote good table manners by setting an example and gives the children the chance to follow that behavior and talk with the other children.

Serve small portions but offer additional servings to meet individual needs. Don't force a child to eat. Young children consume varying amounts of food from day to day and may also have very strong likes and dislikes. Don't use food as a reward or punishment.

Make sure children with special needs receive any particular foods or assistance in eating they may require. Check with the child's parents or health-care professional for specific instructions.

Don't feed the toddlers or preschoolers foods or pieces of food that are the size and shape of a marble. Food this size can be swallowed whole and could become lodged in a child's throat and cause the child to choke. Examples include round slices of hot dogs, whole grapes, marshmallows, chips, and pretzel bits. Cut round objects, such as grapes, melon balls, and marshmallows, in half. Slice hot dogs lengthwise into quarters and then slice across into pieces. You should not give hard candy, dried fruit, popcorn, and other foods that can't be cut into smaller pieces to young children.

Laundry

The laundry area doesn't have to be large, and you don't need commercial equipment to get the job done. Allow approximately 5 to 10 percent of your total space for laundry equipment and supplies. Situate this area close to restroom facilities to take advantage of the existing plumbing.

Place the washer and dryer along the back wall of the room. You may want to have a sink next to the washer for stain removal and other rinsing purposes. Have cabinets installed above the washer and dryer for storage of laundry supplies. If you have room, you may want to include a sorting table where items can be divided by color and care requirements.

Washing machines are available in both top- and front-loading models, and they can handle loads of different sizes. Front-loading washers are usually available in capacities of 18, 25, 35, and 50 pounds. (The weight refers to the dry weight of the clothes being washed.) Top-loaders usually handle smaller loads—usually 12 pounds—than the smallest front-loader and may be preferable if you will be washing primarily smaller loads. Consider energy efficiency and water conservation features when making your selection.

Design and Equipment

The National Resource Center for Health and Safety in Child Care suggests the following standards for equipping laundries in a commercial child-care center:

- You need to have a washing machine and dryer on site or have a contract with a laundry service.
- Laundry equipment should be located in an area separate and secure from the kitchen and child-care areas. Water temperature for laundry equipment should be maintained above 140 degrees unless an approved disinfectant is applied in the rinse cycle (in which case, use the temperature specified by the manufacturer of the chemical), a dryer is used that heats the clothes above 140 degrees, or the clothes are completely ironed. If you use a commercial laundry service, its performance should meet or exceed these requirements for disinfecting.
- Dryers should be vented to the outside.

Buying Used Equipment

Heavy-duty restaurant and laundry hardware does not wear out quickly, so why buy brand-new when seasoned used merchandise can be as good or even better? You can buy secondhand equipment for a fraction of what it would cost new. And there's plenty available from other businesses that have failed, merged or grown to the point where they require larger or more modern equipment.

Buying used equipment is normally a good cost-cutting measure, but there are some pitfalls. Consider that some major equipment has a useful lifetime of only ten years. If you buy a used refrigerator/freezer that is near the end of its useful life, you run the risk of repeated breakdowns, resulting in costly maintenance and food spoilage. Also, newer equipment is generally going to be more cost-efficient to operate. When shopping for used equipment, find out how old it is and factor that into your decision-making. A two-year-old refrigerator for two-thirds the cost of a comparable new unit is probably going to be a much better deal than a nine-year-old refrigerator for one-third of the new price.

Before buying a piece of used equipment, perform a cost analysis of the item you're considering over its expected lifetime vs. that of a comparable new item. When you factor in maintenance and operating costs, there may be circumstances when new equipment may actually be less expensive in the long run.

Look for standard lines of equipment that are both versatile and mobile so you will not have to duplicate hardware. Try to avoid custom-designed lines. Standard equipment is generally less expensive to buy, install, and replace. Also, try to install as much energy-efficient equipment as possible, so long as it's affordable.

Dollar Stretcher

Shopping for used equipment? Don't overlook new-equipment suppliers. They frequently have trade-ins or repossessions that they're willing to sell at discounts of 75 percent or more.

When shopping for used equipment, carefully check it for wear and buy only from reputable dealers. Judicious shopping may turn up some excellent bargains. Check the classified section of your local newspaper for a wide range of used furniture and equipment for sale. Also look under the "Business Opportunities" classification, because businesses that are being liquidated or sold may have fixtures or equipment for sale at substantial savings.

Office
Equipment

Management and administration are critical parts of your operation, and you need the right tools to handle these important tasks. Your office equipment needs will vary significantly depending on the size of your operation. Use the information in this chapter as a guideline, but make your final decision on what to buy based on your situation.

As tempting as it may be to fill your office with an abundance of clever gadgets designed to make your working life easier and more fun, you're better off disciplining yourself to buy only the bare necessities. Consider these primary basic items:

- *Typewriter.* You may think that most typewriters are in museums these days, but they actually remain quite useful to businesses that deal frequently with preprinted and multipart forms, such as contracts and government forms. A good electric typewriter can be purchased for about $100.

- *Computer and printer.* A computer is an essential piece of equipment for a child-care center. It will help you schedule, track staff-to-child ratios, handle the

Beware!
Although multi-functional devices—such as a copier/printer/fax machine or a fax machine/telephone/answering machine—may cost less initially and take up less space in your office than stand-alone items, you'll lose all of these functions simultaneously if the equipment fails. Also, consider the machine's efficiency rating and cost to operate; compare that with stand-alone items before buying.

financial side of your business, and produce policy statements, contracts, and marketing materials. You don't necessarily need the latest and greatest in computer power, but you need a system with the most current version of Windows, a 2.4GHz Pentium 4 processor or Athlon XP 2100+, 512MB to 1GB RAM, an 80GB or larger hard drive, a CD-ROM drive (48X or better), a 56Kbps modem, and a 32MB video card. You should expect to spend $1,500 to $2,000 for your computer, and an additional $100 to $1,000 for a printer. (Color inkjets will run $100 to $500; laser printers range from $300 to $1,000.)

- *Software.* Think of software as your computer's brains, or the instructions that tell your computer how to accomplish the functions you need. There are many programs on the market that will handle your accounting, customer information management, and other administrative requirements. You will also want to take a look at programs designed specifically for child-care centers. (Check the internet.) Software can be a significant investment, so do a careful analysis of your needs, and then study the market and examine a variety of products before making a final decision.

- *Modem.* Modems are necessary to access online services and the internet, and they're a standard component of virtually all computers. If you are going to conduct any business online, whether it's networking with other providers, creating your own web site to attract customers, doing research, or simply communicating via e-mail, you must have a modem. As an alternative to the modem that comes with a computer, you may want to purchase a cable modem (about

$200 plus a monthly fee of about $40); a DSL terminal or modem ($200 to $500, plus a monthly fee of $30 to $40); or an ISDN terminal or modem (about $250 plus $50 per month).

- *Photocopier*. The photocopier is a fixture of the modern office; it's nice to have in a family child-care center and necessary for a commercially located operation. You can get a basic, low-end, no-frills personal copier for $100 to $500 in just about any office supply store. More elaborate models increase proportionately in price. If you anticipate a heavy volume of photocopying (unusual for a homebased or smaller child-care center), consider leasing.

- *Fax machine*. Fax capability has become another must in modern offices. You can either add a fax card to your computer or buy a stand-alone machine. If you use your computer, it must be on to send or receive faxes, and the transmission may interrupt other work. For most businesses, a stand-alone machine on a dedicated telephone line is a wise investment. Expect to pay about $100 for a single-function plain paper fax to $200 to $900 for a multifunction device (fax/copier/printer/scanner).

- *Postage scale*. Unless all your mail is identical, a postage scale is a valuable investment. An accurate scale takes the guesswork out of postage and will quickly pay for itself. It's a good idea to weigh every piece of mail to eliminate the risk of

---

Broken-In or Broken?

Should you buy new equipment, or will used be sufficient? That depends, of course, on which equipment you're thinking about.

For office furniture (desks, chairs, filing cabinets, bookshelves, etc.), you can get some great deals buying used items. You might also be able to save a significant amount of money buying certain office equipment, such as your copier, phone system, and fax machine, used rather than new. However, for high-technology items, such as your computer, you'll probably be better off buying new. Don't try to run your company on outdated technology.

To find good used equipment, you'll need to shop around. Certainly check out used office furniture and equipment dealers. In addition, check the classified section of your local paper under items for sale, as well as notices of bankrupt companies and companies that are going out of business for various reasons and need to liquidate. Also check eBay and other online auctions for new, used, and reconditioned equipment.

items being returned for insufficient postage or overpaying when you are unsure of the weight. Light mailers—one to 12 articles per day—will be adequately served by inexpensive mechanical postal scales, which typically range from $10 to $25. If you are averaging 12 to 24 items per day, consider a digital scale, which is somewhat more expensive—generally from $40 to $200—but significantly more accurate than a mechanical unit. If you send more than 24 items per day or use priority or expedited services frequently, invest in an electronic computing scale, which weighs the item and then calculates the rate via the carrier of your choice, making it easy for you to make comparisons. Programmable electronic scales range from $80 to $250.

> **Bright Idea**
>
> Postage stamps come in a wide array of sizes, designs, and themes, and can add elements of color, whimsy, and even thoughtfulness to mail. Stamps look personal; metered mail looks corporate. Consider using metered mail for invoices, statements, and other official business, and stamps for thank-you notes and marketing correspondence that could use a personal touch.

- *Postage meter.* Postage meters allow you to pay for postage in advance and print the exact amount on the mailing piece. Many postage meters can print in increments of one-tenth of a cent, which can add up to big savings for bulk mail users. Meters also provide a professional image, are more convenient than stamps, and can save you money in a number of ways. Postage meters are leased, not sold, with rates starting at about $20 per month, or you can get a meter/electronic scale combo for $20 to $120 per month. They require a license, which is available from your local post office. Only four manufacturers are licensed by the U.S. Postal Service to manufacture and lease postage meters; your local post office can provide you with contact information.

- *Paper shredder.* A response to both a growing concern for privacy and the need to recycle and conserve space in landfills, shredders are becoming increasingly common in both homes and offices. They allow you to efficiently destroy incoming unsolicited direct mail, as well as sensitive internal documents, such as children's records, before they are discarded. Shredded paper can be compacted much more tightly than paper tossed in a wastebasket, which conserves landfill space. Light-duty shredders start at about $25, and heavier-capacity shredders run $80 to $180.

- *Credit and debit card processing equipment.* This could range from a simple imprint machine to an online terminal. Consult with several merchant status providers to determine the most appropriate and cost-effective equipment for your business.

Telecommunications

The ability to communicate quickly with your customers, employees, and suppliers is essential to any business. Advancing technology gives you a wide range of telecommunications options. Most telephone companies have created departments dedicated to small and homebased businesses. Contact your local service provider and ask to speak with someone who can review your needs and help you put together a service and equipment package that will work for you. Specific elements to keep in mind include:

- *Telephone.* Whether you're homebased or in a commercial location, you should have two voice telephone lines. If you plan to grow and your call volume increases, you can add more lines.

  Your telephone can be a tremendous productivity tool, and most of the models on the market today are rich in features you will find useful. Such features include automatic redial, which redials the last number called at regular intervals until the call is completed; programmable memory for storing frequently called numbers; and speakerphone for hands-free use. You may also want call forwarding, which allows you to forward calls to another number when you're not at your desk, and call waiting, which signals you that another call is coming in while you are on the phone. These services are typically available through your telephone company for a monthly fee.

  If you are going to be spending a great deal of time on the phone, perhaps doing marketing or handling customer service, consider using a headset for comfort and efficiency. A cordless phone lets you move around freely while talking, but these units vary widely in price and quality, so research them thoroughly before making a purchase.

- *Answering machine/voice mail.* Because your business phone should never go unanswered, you will need some sort of reliable answering device to take calls when you can't do it yourself. Whether you buy an answering machine (expect to pay $15 to $65 for a basic model or $100 to $200 for one with advanced features) or use the voice-mail service provided through your telephone company depends on your personal preferences, work style, and needs.

- *Cellular phone.* Once considered a luxury, cellular phones are almost as common as landlines and have even replaced landlines for many users. Most have features similar to your office phone—such as caller ID, call waiting, and voice mail—and equipment

> **Bright Idea**
>
> If you're homebased, have a private telephone line only your friends know about; this lets you feel comfortable answering the phone during evenings and weekends, knowing that it will not be a parent calling to talk about their children.

and service packages are very reasonably priced. Cellular phones are essential if you're going to be transporting children. The average price for a phone plus service is $39.99 a month.

- *Pager*. A pager lets you know that someone is trying to reach you and lets you decide when to return the call. Many people use pagers in conjunction with cellular phones to conserve the cost of air time. Ask prospective pager suppliers if your system can be set up so you are paged whenever someone leaves a message in your voice-mail box. This service allows you to retrieve your messages immediately and eliminates having to periodically check to see if anyone has called. As with cellular phones, the pager industry is very competitive, so shop around for the best deal. Expect to pay about $72 per year.

- *E-mail*. E-mail is a standard element in a company's communication package. It allows for fast, efficient, trackable 24-hour communication and is a great way for you to conduct nonemergency communication with parents. Check your messages regularly and reply to them promptly. E-mail costs range from free to $25 per month.

Keep Your Customers Out of Voice-Mail Jail

Voice mail is one of the most popular modern business conveniences and can be a significant communication tool. Even so, whenever possible, answer your phone yourself—and insist that your employees do likewise. Handle calls as quickly and efficiently as possible. When parents call with a question or concern about their children, they want to speak to a person, not a recording device.

Some other things to keep in mind: The prices of automated answering systems are dropping so much that even very small businesses can afford them. If you use an automated answering system, be sure to tell callers how to reach a live person. Ideally, that information should come very early in your announcement. For example, your greeting might sound something like this:

Thank you for calling ABC Child Care. If you know the extension of the person you are calling,

Tip...

Smart Tip

Resist the temptation to fritter away time on your computer. The abundance of easy-to-use software on the market today gives us fun ways to turn out impressive documents, tempting you and your employees to add artwork, color, and even motion to your materials. While a certain amount of creativity helps your competitive position, take care that it doesn't get out of control and become a serious time-waster.

you may enter it now. To reach an operator, dial zero at any time during this message. If your child is enrolled in our center and you need to speak to someone, press one. To schedule a tour of our facility, press two. For information on our hours and location, press three. For accounting, press four. For a center directory, press five.

Whether you're a one-person show or you have a sizable staff, change your individual voice-mail announcements daily. Callers need to know whether you're in the office or out and whether they're likely to hear back from you in five minutes or five hours. Avoid stating the obvious, such as "I'm either away from my desk or out of the office"—well, of course! If you were at your desk, you'd be answering your phone. And always let callers know how to reach a live person when you are not available. Here is a sample individual voice-mail announcement:

"This is Jane Smith, and it's Monday, June 1st. I'm in the office today but unavailable at the moment. Leave your name, number, and the reason for your call, and I'll get back to you within an hour. If you need to speak with someone immediately, press zero and ask the operator to connect you with Bob White."

Office Supplies

Because what you sell is a service, you will require very little in the way of office supplies—but what you need to keep on hand is important.

You'll need to be sure to maintain an adequate stock of marketing materials, including brochures, sales items, etc. You will also need to maintain an ample supply of administrative items, including checks, invoices, receipts, stationery, paper, and miscellaneous office supplies.

Local stationers and office supply stores will have most or all the miscellaneous office supplies you need. You may even find some items in your child-care equipment and supply catalogs. Take a look at the "Office Supplies Checklist" on page 110 to get started.

Office Supplies Checklist

In addition to office equipment, you'll need an assortment of minor office supplies. Those items include:

❑ Scratch pads

❑ Staplers, staples, and staple removers

❑ Tape and dispensers

❑ Scissors

❑ "Sticky" notes in an assortment of sizes

❑ Paper clips

❑ Plain paper for your copier and printer

❑ Paper and other supplies for your fax machine (if you have one)

❑ Letter openers

❑ Pens, pencils, and holders

❑ Correction fluid (to correct typewritten or handwritten documents)

❑ Trash cans

❑ Desktop document trays

Transportation
Services

Children won't magically show up at your
door—they have to be transported there, usually by car. Some
child-care providers leave the issue of transportation entirely up
to the parents; others offer various transportation services. In
fact, some entrepreneurs decide to skip the child-care center and

focus their businesses on providing transportation to children whose parents are unable to shuttle them around.

Many requirements regarding transporting children are the same whether you're doing it as an adjunct to your child-care center or as your primary business. We'll take a look at the basics you need to know when you're transporting children for any reason and then cover additional issues involved in starting a kids' transportation service.

Regulations regarding providing transportation for a fee vary from state to state, and even by local jurisdiction. For example, your state may not require any special licensing, but your county or city might. When varying standards apply, you should meet the more restrictive one. And be sure you have everything you need in the way of licenses and permits before you start operating.

> **Smart Tip** — Tip...
>
> Though not required by law, each vehicle transporting children should have a cellular phone so you can easily call for help in the event of a crash, breakdown, or other emergency. This way, you won't have to leave the children unsupervised or undersupervised for any length of time.

Driver Requirements

Drivers should hold a current state driver's license authorizing them to drive the particular type of vehicle and to transport children. They should have a clean driving record. Of course, you need to be reasonable. One ticket for a moving violation over a three-year period doesn't mean a person is a reckless driver; however, several tickets and/or chargeable accidents would preclude you from hiring someone.

Check the state's criminal record file and child abuse registry as part of your employee background check on drivers. No person with a record of abusing children or with a criminal record of crimes of violence or sexual molestation should be allowed to transport children. You might also want to run a workers' compensation claim check to see if the individual has a record of on-the-job injuries.

Vehicle Requirements

All your vehicles should be licensed and registered according to the laws of your state.

When the temperature exceeds 75 degrees, vehicles should be air-conditioned; when the temperature drops below 50 degrees, vehicles should be heated. Drivers should be instructed on this requirement, and the policy should also be visibly posted in the vehicle.

Each vehicle should be equipped with a first-aid kit. In addition to the items in your facility first-aid kit (see Chapter 7 for a list), your vehicle kit should include a bottle of water, soap, coins for a pay telephone, and a first-aid guide. You should also have a road

Dollar Stretcher

Shop around for automotive service sources. One-stop shopping may be convenient, but it often isn't cost-efficient. Consider using a variety of mechanics who specialize in different aspects of vehicle maintenance. Whether you use one or more resources for vehicle maintenance, be sure it's someone you can trust and who understands how important it is to keep your vehicles safe on the road.

emergency safety kit, which includes warning triangle and flares, fix-a-flat, oil, and minor mechanical tools and supplies.

Emergency identification and contact information for all children being transported should be in the vehicle in case of an injury or illness.

You may want to consider equipping your vehicles with tracking devices to protect against theft and unauthorized use. Though this isn't a requirement, it could be a tremendous advantage.

Training

All drivers, passenger monitors, and assistants should receive instruction in child passenger safety precautions, including the use of safety restraints, handling of emergency situations, route training, defensive driving, and child supervision responsibilities. They should also be certified in pediatric first aid, including rescue breathing and first aid for choking. That an individual, whether a paid staff member or a volunteer, has received such instruction and earned any certifications should be documented in his or her personnel records.

General Policies

The following are some general policies you'll want to adopt for your children's transportation business.

- Do not allow smoking in any of the vehicles used by your facility at any time. Post a "No Smoking" sign in each vehicle. Children with respiratory problems and allergies will suffer health consequences if they're exposed to secondhand smoke, even indirectly. Prohibiting smoking in the vehicles makes it easier to keep them clean.

- Drivers should not have consumed alcohol within 12 hours prior to transporting children. The use of illegal drugs by drivers should also be prohibited. If you suspect noncompliance with these issues, you should require drug testing of your employees.

- Any prescription drugs taken by drivers should not impair their ability to provide safe transportation. Drivers should be instructed to advise their healthcare provider at the time of prescription that they operate a motor vehicle that transports children and question whether or not it is safe to do so while on the medication.

- Do not allow loud radio or music playing in the vehicle; post a sign conveying this policy. Loud noise may be disturbing to children with central nervous system abnormalities as well as distracting to the driver and the passenger monitor or assistant attending to the children in the vehicle. Drivers should also be prohibited from using headphones to listen to music or other kinds of distracting sounds while children are in the vehicles.

- When children are driven in a motor vehicle other than a bus or school bus and operated by a common carrier (whether or not you are considered a common carrier will be determined by your state Department of Transportation), each child must be fastened in an approved safety seat, seat belt, or harness appropriate to the child's weight. The restraint must be installed and used in accordance with the manufacturer's instructions. Each child must have an individual seat belt or other appropriate restraint.

- Children under the age of 4 should be transported only if they are securely fastened in a child passenger restraining system that meets the federal motor vehicle safety standards contained in the Code of Federal Regulations, Title 49, Section 571.213, and this compliance is indicated on the safety restraint device.

- If small buses or vans have safety belts installed, they must be used by the children.

- All drivers should know and keep in the vehicle the quickest route to the nearest hospital from any point on their routes.

- Children should not be transported for more than one hour per one-way trip. It is unreasonable to expect very young children to remain confined and seated for more than one hour.

- Have enough providers present to make sure that proper child-to-provider ratios are maintained. Do not count the driver as a provider; a driver is not able to properly supervise children while driving the vehicle.

- Never leave a child unsupervised in a vehicle.

- Decide how much notice you will require for service. The difference between a typical children's transportation service and a taxi is that you can call a taxi at the last minute—of course, it may or may not arrive when you need it. A good policy is

> **Beware!**
> Children's transportation is a seasonal business. Unless you're in an area with year-round schools, you can expect to have a major drop in income over the summer. You can reduce your staff, but much of your overhead expenses (vehicle payments, insurance, etc.) will continue, so set aside money during your busy times to cover your costs when revenue is down.

to ask for two days' notice, but be willing to work with regular customers when they have a last-minute request.

- Develop a plan that is communicated to all staff and parents for the safe pickup and drop-off of children. Your plan should include pickup and drop-off only at a curb or an off-street location that is protected from traffic. A responsible adult should supervise children during boarding and exiting and should make sure each child is buckled into a seat restraint before the vehicle moves and is clear of the vehicle's path after exiting.

Bright Idea

The fastest and easiest way to establish and grow a children's transportation service is to target affluent schools that do not provide their own bus services. You can easily find those schools listed in the telephone directory, and a quick call will give you the information you need.

- The driver should also wait to make sure the child is safely inside the destination and that an authorized adult is on the premises. If no authorized adult is there, don't leave the child until the parent is notified of the situation and approves it.

- For additional security and safety, assign each customer a personal identification number (PIN), which they must provide if they are calling to make any changes to a child's schedule or to who is authorized to receive the child.

- If your customers are involved in custody disputes or other situations where there are court orders regarding contact, ask for a copy of the order and keep it in the vehicle when the child is on board. If the parent, or other person who is being denied visitation, attempts to see the child, you (or your driver) can immediately call the police and produce the court order so appropriate action can be taken.

- You may want to consider requiring uniforms for drivers. It will make your operation look more professional and increase the comfort level of both parents and passengers if drivers are easily identifiable.

Children Will Be Children

Keep in mind that you're transporting youngsters, not adults, and establish policies to assure the safety of all the children while in your vehicles. If you know that certain children have personality conflicts with others, seat them apart. Establish behavioral rules and enforce them. If there is an actual altercation, notify the parent. Depending on the seriousness of the incident, or if it happens more than once, refuse to transport the child. You may also run into a situation with an older child (perhaps early teens) resisting the idea of using a children's transportation service, or you may have passengers who don't want to go where their parents want them to go. Doris McNeill, owner of Kids on Wheels Inc. in Gainesville, Florida, recalls a time when a seventh-grade girl decided she didn't want Kids on Wheels to take her to her after-school activities. Instead, she wanted to go home after school, where she would have been unsupervised for several hours a day. She started telling her mother negative things about the service that weren't true. McNeill tried to work things out, but she says, "She ended up not using our services anymore, and started taking the school bus home like the big girl she thought she was. Kids are going to be kids, and we run into this sort of thing occasionally."

Starting a Transportation Service

Private children's transportation is a growing industry. As more parents enter the workforce, the demand for safe transportation of children to and from school, medical appointments, sports events, and other activities will continue to grow. Also, many private schools prefer to use an outside transportation provider rather than do it themselves to reduce their liability.

If you're interested in starting a children's transportation service, your first step is to check with your state Department of Transportation to find out what regulations apply. Most states don't have legislation or regulations targeted directly to this industry, so it's

---

Fuel for Thought

Gasoline prices are the most unpredictable variable for transportation companies. A sharp increase in gas prices that's not offset by higher fees can seriously erode your profits. But because most of your services are provided under the terms of a contract (monthly, quarterly, semiannually, or annually), you can't arbitrarily raise prices.

Solve this problem by placing a fuel surcharge in your contract allowing you to increase charges when fuel prices go up. Make your surcharge a percent per rider, not a flat fee per client, since many clients will be using your service for more than one child, and the increase in fees should be based on consumption. Also, you may want to link your increase to a specific gas price (such as, "when regular gas prices exceed $X per gallon") because customers will be more comfortable if the surcharge is not an arbitrary decision you can make without notifying them.

important that you be clear and specific about what you're planning to do. You should also check with your city or county (and any other jurisdictions in which you plan to operate) to see what sort of regulations are in place.

Depending on the size of the operation you start, you will need as much as $50,000 to $60,000 in investment capital to get started and to cover your expenses for the first two years or so until you become profitable. McNeill traded in her personal car for a van and was able to start with just a few thousand dollars cash.

Do the same sort of market research you would do for any new business. Ideally, you'll need to serve a population base of at least 75,000. You might be able to build a small business in a less populated area, but it will be difficult. You'll also need to target areas with household incomes of $70,000 or more. While almost everyone with children needs and wants your service, the reality is that lower-income families can't afford it.

Bright Idea

Consider letting your drivers take their vans home at night. This accomplishes two important things: It relieves you of having to deal with overnight parking of commercial vehicles (which may be a problem if you're homebased), and it solves any personal transportation problems your drivers might have. Gainesville, Florida, entrepreneur Doris McNeill says it also makes it easier on the drivers when they have very early pickups. You may want to restrict use of the vans to commuting and not allow any other personal use.

When you're starting out, keep your operation contained within a radius of 8 to 12 miles. After a couple years, as you grow and gain experience, you can expand your geographical service area.

Target institutional or corporate clients for the core of your business. Places such as child-care centers, preschools, before- and after-school programs, private schools, YMCAs, and even your local school board are good sources. Of course, individual contracts are important and can be very profitable; they just aren't quite as reliable as institutions.

A children's transportation business can be started from home with just one or two vehicles. However, if you're planning to operate from home, be sure you have a place to park commercially marked vehicles; many communities have restrictions as to the number and type of vehicles that can be parked at a residence overnight.

When it comes to choosing vehicles for your business, keep in mind that minivans are not necessarily the best choice. They are not cost-effective for commercial transportation and are very difficult to operate at a profit. Take your time and shop carefully for your vehicles to get the best combination of cost to operate and safety. Also, McNeill advises, keep detailed records on maintenance and costs.

Setting Prices

Use a formula of labor plus overhead plus profit (see "Setting Prices" in Chapter 5) to calculate your transportation fees. Your first year will take a lot of guesswork, but it will get easier once you have some actual numbers to track.

Estimate your costs—labor, expenses, and overhead—and then add your desired profit. McNeill says the passenger transportation industry averages a 15 to 20 percent profit margin. Then estimate how many riders you can realistically serve and what type of service (one-way, round-trip, special trip) they will need. This will give you an idea of the minimum your average rider should be paying so you have a center point to make sure you're not undercharging. When estimating expenses, be generous with your figures, because it will often cost you more to operate than you think it will.

One of the easiest ways to calculate fees is on a per-mile basis. You might charge a minimum that includes up to a certain number of miles, then a per-mile rate above that.

Choose Your Vehicles Carefully

They are popular with schools, churches, day-care centers, and children's transportation services, but the National Transportation Safety Board (NTSB) reports 1,441 fatal crashes involving 15-passenger vans between 1990 and 2001. A major problem with these vehicles is that their tires are often under-inflated, which leads to higher tire temperature, faster tire deterioration, and diminished driving stability, often causing the vehicle to roll over. When selecting vehicles for transporting children, study safety and crash records. Many transportation providers are replacing 15-passenger vans with miniature school buses and other vehicles for safety reasons.

Safety experts at the NTSB offer these tips for safety in 15-passenger vans (and other vehicles, as well):

○ Wear seat belts. Keep all seat belts accessible, and require that all passengers use them.

○ Inspect seat belts regularly and keep them in good working order.

○ Check the tire pressure often and make sure it conforms to the van and tire manufacturers' standards.

○ Be aware that front and back tires may require different inflation pressures.

○ Routinely check the condition of tires for uneven wear, cracks, and damage, and replace them if necessary.

○ Do not overload 15-passenger vans, and do not use a roof rack. As the weight inside a van increases, so does the van's propensity for rollover.

Your rate structure should also include a provision for cancellation; typically, trips that are canceled without a certain amount of notice should be billed.

Hiring and Keeping Drivers

Finding qualified drivers who can pass your background check and who are willing to work the hours required will be one of your biggest challenges. The fact that transporting children is a seasonal business and most drivers will work a split shift can add to the challenge of finding and keeping good people. During the school year, it's common for children's transportation drivers to typically work from 6 A.M. to 9 A.M. and then from 2 P.M. to 6 P.M.

As you grow, study your driver turnover pattern. When drivers leave, take the time to find out why. Always be recruiting, even when you don't have any openings. You never know when someone will leave or you'll need to expand, and you should always have a pool of strong candidates to choose from.

At first glance, it might seem that mothers who want to work part time would be good candidates, but this is not the case. The times when mothers need to be with their kids, such as early in the morning before school or in the afternoon after school, are the times your drivers will be working. McNeill advises cross-training your drivers so at least two people are familiar with every route. If you're a solo operator, have someone you can call as a backup if you get sick or your vehicle breaks down. "Your drivers become like family," McNeill says. "You get to know them and who they hang out with. That's important to me."

Before the First Ride

When you get a new client, have a personal meeting with the child and parents to complete all the necessary paperwork and to go over your policies. McNeill suggests bringing the person who will be the actual driver along to that meeting, especially when the child is very young. "We teach safety and to not go to strangers, so make sure the child knows you," she advises. Children should be told to only get into a vehicle that is clearly marked as one of yours. "I try to bring the vehicle the child will be picked up in. I take them outside and say, 'OK, this is what you're looking for.'"

Expect to build the same sort of relationship with the kids you transport as a child-care provider does. "I'm like one of the relatives—Aunt Doris," McNeill says. "I'll be out somewhere and see kids I haven't transported in years, and they'll come up and give me a big hug."

At the same time, professionalism is essential. "Anybody can go pick up a child," McNeill says. "What's going to make a person want to pull out their checkbook after they meet you?" The appearance of your drivers and vehicles, plus your contracts and policy documents, all combine to create an image that is the key to your success.

11

Parent
Relationships

Children, caregivers, parents, and administrators can all benefit from positive relationships between the parents and child-care providers. The foundation of such relationships is a frequent exchange of information about the child's strengths, progress, and needed changes.

One thing you are most likely to have in common with the parents of the children in your care is a lack of time. Everyone is pressured by the demands of work and home. Though you may feel that the time involved in writing notes, making phone calls to parents, arranging parent/caregiver conferences, and allowing parents to visit the center takes away from the time you spend doing your work, it actually does not. These efforts can generate tremendous rewards. Take the time to share a personal observation about the child with a hurried parent, and perhaps offer a cup of coffee and a chance to pause for a moment and focus on the child. Of course, respect the parents' schedule constraints by choosing convenient times to make these contacts.

Parents often, and justifiably, have very strong ideas about how their children should be cared for. While you must respect a parent's wishes, it is impossible to comply with every parent's particular style of child-raising. For example, some parents are firmly in favor of physically punishing their children for misbehaving. However, for legal reasons (at the very least—you may also have other reasons), you should have a clear policy of never striking or physically punishing any child. The legal definitions of child abuse are hazy at best, and even the appearance or accusation of abuse can destroy a child-care center. Make your disciplinary limitation explicit to your staff, and inform parents of your firm policy as well.

Parents also might want to have frequent progress reports during the day, calling in two or three times or even expecting your staff to find time to make frequent calls. Whether you want to make such calls or you have a policy of only calling in the event of an emergency, make it clear that you will accept a call from a parent or guardian at any time. It takes little effort to provide this reassuring service, and abuses of it will be rare.

Bright Idea

Remember that the children's parents are your customers and need to be thanked for their business. Consider ideas such as hosting an annual parent appreciation dinner at a moderately priced restaurant or giving modest holiday gifts. Even a periodic handwritten thank-you note will let the parents know you recognize their role in your business success.

Encouraging Parental Involvement

Most parents want to be involved in child-care activities, and as a provider, it is up to you to offer ways to make it easy for them to do so. When parents are involved in their children's lives at the child-care facility, they benefit in a wide variety of ways, but particularly in an improved and closer relationship with their children. As the provider, you'll benefit from having parents serve on your advisory board or on committees.

At your initial meeting with parents, outline your program and emphasize the importance of

Smart Tip

Be prepared to educate young parents, especially single mothers. "A lot of young mothers are open to suggestions," says Janet Hale, owner of Gingerbread House. "We don't want to intrude, and we respect their family relationship, but if we can instruct them on how to do something better, we often will."

parental involvement. You should communicate regularly with the parents through informal and formal written notices, and try to talk with each parent at least once a week. If a discipline problem develops, involve the parents early to prevent a minor problem from becoming a major issue.

Plan family activities such as picnics and dinners. Invite parents to stop by the center for lunch or to join their children for various special events you may hold. Be sure the parents know they are welcome to come by anytime—whether or not something special is happening.

You may also want to sponsor educational programs designed to help improve parent-child relationships. This promotes parental involvement as well as strengthens your relationship with parents and can also serve as a marketing tool if you open the programs to the community.

Lois Mitten Rosenberry in Toledo, Ohio, says the key is to develop a mindset of always looking for ways to support the parent. Her centers have a parents' council that all parents are encouraged to join. Staff members are conscientious about being available to parents who have concerns or just want to talk about their children. And as the caregivers and administrators learn about the families, they are able to strengthen the bonds. "If you know someone is in the hospital, you send a card or a teddy bear. You ask how an elderly parent is doing [many parents of young children are also caring for their own elderly parents]," says Mitten Rosenberry. "It's the communication and just reaching out in a personal way."

Keeping Parents Informed

You may spend more waking hours with the children in your care than their parents do, and parents will appreciate knowing what their children are doing during that time.

Consider keeping a notebook on each child. It could include a daily log of the child's activities, including how many bowel movements and a description of the feces, how many wet diapers, what and how much food he or she consumed, his or her nap schedule, and anything else that pertains to the child. If you have any questions

Smart Tip

Be particularly sensitive to new mothers who are leaving small babies in a child-care facility for the first time. If they are allowed to receive calls at work, call them with updates during the day so they know all is well with their child. Or if it's more practical, send them e-mail updates.

for the parent, note them in the log. Have the parents take the notebook home at night and bring it back in the morning.

For minor bumps and bruises that do not require serious medical attention, Janet Hale in Exeter, California, completes an "Ouchy" Report (see page 125), which is sent home with the child at the end of the day. She or a staff member gives the parent a daily verbal report when the child is picked up.

You may also want to produce a newsletter telling parents about activities at the center and discussing other important issues. For example, if you are homebased, you may need to occasionally remind parents to be considerate of your neighbors when they are dropping off and picking up their children, and a newsletter is a nonconfrontational way to do that.

Helping Parents Understand Your Bond with Their Children

Ideally, the children in your care will form close bonds with you or their particular caregivers. Such attachments may make some parents uneasy, but they're an important part of the child's development and learning and in no way detract from the bonds children have with their parents and other family members. Children need to view their outside care and education settings as safe places where adults other than their parents support and care for them. You need to work with parents to make this happen.

Explain to parents that it's important to mention the caregiver's name in conversations at home and to show interest in their child's interactions with that person. When dropping children off at the child-care facility, parents should say goodbye in a confident and nonchalant manner. They also need to be prepared for the fact that there will be times when the child does not want to go home at the end of the day and may even

A Picture Is Worth a Thousand Words

One simple effort can strengthen your relationship with parents and be a valuable marketing tool, says Lois Mitten Rosenberry. At Children's Discovery Centers and Discovery Express in Toledo, Ohio, on a child's first day, the youngster's picture is taken. It's placed in an inexpensive frame with the center's logo on it and sent to the parent's office along with a note telling the parent what the child did that day. If the parent leaves the picture out on his or her desk—and just about all of them do—the center's name and logo is there for other working parents to see. And parents appreciate the gesture.

"Ouchy" Report

Your child,

_____ ,

had an "ouchy" today at

_____ a.m./p.m.

He/she _____

_____

and we _____

_____

If you have any questions,
please ask me.

_____
signature of child-care employee

Courtesy: Gingerbread House, Exeter, California

cry about being forced to leave the center. Explain that this is normal, and although they may feel rejected as parents, it doesn't mean their children do not love them.

If You Have a Problem

Problems and disagreements with parents and children are bound to occur every so often. Address them as soon as possible; don't let them fester and grow into major issues.

Bring the situation to the parent's attention when neither of you is tired—and when you both have time for a discussion. If that time isn't available during your normal contacts when the child is being dropped off or picked up, set an appointment. Talk in a polite, positive manner, without casting blame. Ask for the parent's help or advice. For example, if a child seems to be unusually tired, don't say something like, "You need to put her to bed earlier." Instead, try an approach like, "Jennifer seems to be more tired than normal lately. Is she having trouble sleeping?"

Let the parents know that you are their ally, not their adversary. At the same time, you want to make it clear that certain situations cannot be tolerated. If you have a child who isn't behaving to the extent that the other children are unhappy, you must correct the problem. For example, if you have a child who hits and/or bites, you'll quickly find that other parents don't want to leave their kids in a place where they might be hit or bitten. For the sake of your business, as well as for the sake of the child, work closely with the parents to correct bad behavior. Always keep in mind that parents will find it easier to accept discussions on problems and your suggestions for improvement if they know you see their child's good points, too. There will be times when a problem will be resolved with just one conversation, and there will be other times when the situation will require many conferences and plenty of joint effort to resolve. As you work through the negatives, remember to comment sincerely on helpful things the parents are doing for their child.

When a Parent Has a Problem

When a parent comes to you with a problem or complaint, listen carefully—not just to the words but to what isn't being said. Though you might feel like you are under attack or are being unfairly criticized, try not to react defensively or let hurt or anger get the best of you. Hear the parent out, and remember that he or she is your customer and has a right to express his or her feelings and opinions about the services you provide. In fact, the complaint may well provide you with input you can use to improve your operation.

Once a parent has presented an issue and finished talking, repeat what you think you heard. Say something like, "I want to make sure I understand your concerns. What you're saying is..." and then summarize what was said and ask for a confirmation that your interpretation is accurate. If it's not, let the parent speak again, and then go through the clarification process one more time to be sure you understand.

After you are sure you are both talking about the same thing, share your thoughts and feelings about the problem. Ask the parent for input and suggestions. Together, you should be able to come up with several possible solutions and then decide which approach to take to remedy the situation.

Sometimes you will have problems that simply can't be solved. Don't blame yourself if, in spite of your best efforts, things just don't work out. It may be the result of a personality clash, differences in beliefs about child-rearing, or unrealistic demands made on you or the child. It doesn't mean you're not a good child-care provider, just that you and this particular client are mismatched.

Beware!
Always enforce your late pickup policies, even when the parent has a good reason or is usually on time. If you let it slide once or twice and then begin enforcing the rules, the parents will be both confused and offended. Consistency is as important with the parents as it is with the children.

When Parents Are Chronically Late

One of the most frustrating aspects of being a child-care professional is parents who are late picking up their children. Before you accept a family, make sure they understand your hours of operation and that their work schedules are compatible with yours.

It's possible some parents don't realize they are causing a problem when they are late, especially if you are a family (homebased) center or a commercial center with extended or nontraditional hours. They may not be aware that their tardiness creates a conflict for you.

For parents who are occasionally late, simply follow your policy guidelines regarding fees. After all, there will always be circumstances that will periodically cause delays.

When parents are chronically late, explain how their actions are affecting you, your employees, your family, and/or the other children in your care. You might say something like, "When you are late, it keeps me from getting home to my own family." Or "Because you were late, I was late to an important meeting." Or, if you are open extended hours, try, "We are required by law to have no more than a certain number of children for each caregiver on duty. When you are late, we are forced to violate that ratio. It means the children aren't getting adequate care, and it also puts our license in jeopardy." Then ask how the two of you can work together to solve the problem.

You might also point out how the parents' behavior affects their child. Children usually find it stressful when their routine is changed. They are also likely to react negatively to being the only child left at the center and will undoubtedly pick up on any stress the caregiver is feeling due to the situation. Also, children worry when their parents are late. Parents may not realize the impact of their tardiness on everyone involved, and they may make more of an effort to be on time if you explain it to them.

Communication Tips

One of the biggest challenges in all human relationships is communication. Child-care providers may experience rocky relationships with parents because of different experiences, belief systems, and simply an inability to understand the other's perspective. You should address these issues in your pre-enrollment meeting, but communication is an ongoing process. These tips will help:

- Do not gossip. Refuse to listen to negative information about others, particularly previous providers.
- Listen carefully to what parents are saying about their children. Ask for clarification when necessary.
- Figure out what parents are asking you to do and why before you make a decision on whether it is possible and/or reasonable.
- Explain your position.

- Avoid coming across as defensive.
- Focus on the common ground rather than differences.
- Learn from each other.
- Be open to trying the parents' suggestions—after all, this is their child.
- Share good events of the day.
- Smile—you will look better and feel better.
- Report any accidents, no matter how minor, and explain how they happened. Parents understand that scrapes and bumps are part of growing up.
- Be available and understanding.
- Keep all personal information confidential.
- Don't talk about a child's problem in front of that child, any other child, or any other parent. Set up a time to discuss the issue privately with the child's parents.
- You should take a genuine interest in the parents and their lives apart from the direct issues that are relative to their children.

12

Marketing

In most parts of the United States, the demand for quality child care is so high that marketing your business will be relatively easy. In fact, many of the providers we talked to for this book—especially the homebased centers—do little or no marketing because they are established, with strong reputations and waiting lists. But every business needs a marketing plan, and yours is no exception.

There are issues and ideas specific to child-care and child transportation services that you need to know as you develop your plan. For example, the tips in the previous chapter on relationships with parents are not only good from an operational standpoint, but they will also aid your marketing efforts. You should also check with your local phone company to find out its advertising deadline and directory distribution date and, if possible, plan to launch your business in time to be included. Your Yellow Pages listing will be an important source of new business, especially in the early days, so don't get so distracted by other start-up tasks that you miss this opportunity. Another telephone directory issue is that if you're starting a children's transportation service, you may find that your book doesn't include a classification for you. And even if it does, you might also want to include your company under the sections for child-care and transportation services.

All your marketing materials should be professional and letter-perfect. Consider hiring a graphic designer and/or professional writer to help you with your marketing package. If they have children, you may be able to negotiate a trade-off.

Keep these questions in mind as you form your marketing plan:

- Who are your potential customers?
- How many of them are there?
- Where are they located?
- What are they currently doing for child care?
- Can you offer them anything they are not getting now?
- How can you persuade them to bring their children to you?
- Exactly what services do you offer?
- How do you compare with your competitors?
- What kind of image do you want to project?

The goal of your marketing plan should be to convey your existence and the quality of your service to prospective customers, ideally using a multifaceted approach. The child-care center operators we talked with used a variety of marketing methods, from simple word-of-mouth to more sophisticated techniques.

Lois Mitten Rosenberry has advertised in local Toledo, Ohio, newspapers and on radio, provided real estate agents with information packets for new people moving into the community, given gift bags to churches for new mothers, held open houses, passed out fliers, used billboards, and attended children's fairs. "Our most effective [ways of gaining new clients], however, are simple parent referrals, drive-bys, and Yellow Pages [ads]," she says.

Janet Hale does some newspaper advertising in Exeter, California, and has even done floats in parades but finds fliers and word-of-mouth work best.

After-School Special

After-school care includes programs for school-age children for those hours they are not in school but while their parents are working. Unfortunately, in many areas, the number of programs available for these children falls far short of meeting the demand. Conversely, as a private provider, you may find yourself in the position of having to justify the cost of your service to parents who are struggling on their own tight budgets. The following information will help you sell your service:

○ The rate of violent juvenile crime triples during the hours of 3 P.M. and 8 P.M., according to a recent report made to the U.S. attorney general.

○ On school days, the hours between 3 P.M. and 6 P.M. are the peak times for teens to commit crimes, be victims of crimes, be in or cause a car crash, and smoke, drink, or use drugs.

○ Children are most likely to be victims of a violent crime by a nonfamily member between the hours of 2 P.M. and 6 P.M., according to the Office of Juvenile Justice and Delinquency Prevention.

○ A study of eighth-graders who were unsupervised beginning in elementary and junior high school found that children without adult supervision are at significantly greater risk of truancy from school, stress, receiving poor grades, risk-taking behavior, and substance abuse.

○ A number of studies have found that children who attend quality programs have better peer relations, social skills, emotional adjustment, grades, and conduct in school compared with their peers who are not in programs. They also have more learning opportunities and academic or enrichment activities, and spend less time watching television.

○ Teachers and principals report that students become more cooperative, learn to better handle conflicts, develop an interest in recreational reading, and receive better grades due to participation in after-school programs, according to a study recently conducted by the University of Wisconsin.

For Kids on Wheels, Doris McNeill has a web site and newsletter. Her brightly painted van is also very effective advertising. For a children's transportation service, you may also want to use direct mail by building a list from school directories.

Direct Mail

Because of the ability to target well-defined geographical areas, direct mail can be a very effective way to promote your child-care center. It also allows you to send a personalized sales message.

The best methods for direct-mail advertising of a child-care center are personal sales letters and brochures. Use a solo mailer, rather than including your information in a cooperative mailer that is full of supermarket coupons and the like. Parents don't select child care the way they choose barbecue sauce, so the less expensive cooperative mailer can cost you the professional image that you can effectively create through a solo mailer.

In your mailer, you might want to include a reply card that allows the prospective customer a chance to ask for more information or for you to contact them to arrange a tour.

A sales letter will allow you to add an effective personal touch. It should be personal, written in an informal style, and selectively directed.

Start your letter with something that will grab the prospect's attention. It might be a description of a special offer or the benefits of your child-care center. It may flatter the reader or tell a story. Here are two possible ways to open your letter:

1. "When my children were young, quality day care was virtually nonexistent. Families were faced with the choice of teenage baby-sitters, imposing on nearby relatives, or having one parent stay at home until the child was old enough to be left alone. With KidLand Child Care, I have created a new alternative: a well-supervised, challenging, and enriching atmosphere that provides the safe, fun, and stimulating environment most beneficial to young children."

2. "Like most parents of young children, you've probably had to seriously weigh your child's need for a safe and enriching environment with the economic necessity of working full time. Images of a child parked in front of the television for six hours while the baby-sitter talks on the phone haunt many parents today. Fortunately, there is a better option, one that provides your child an enriching social and educational environment that is fully supervised by qualified caregivers—KidLand Child Care."

The body copy of your letter should let the prospect know the exact reason you are writing and what you have to offer. Headlines in letters can be very effective, but if you use one, it should describe the main benefit you are trying to promote. Expand on that point throughout the letter, reiterating that specific benefit as often as you can, using different descriptions so the reader will remember that benefit.

> **Bright Idea**
>
> In your direct mail, emphasize the importance of choosing quality child care. In your marketing materials, include tips on what parents should look for in a provider.

Any claims you make should be qualified by citing sources or offering endorsements. You should also include what the reader will lose if they don't respond—for example, indicate that you only have a few openings available and they are filling up fast—and then close your letter with a repeat of the main benefit and a "call to action," which tells the reader what they should do next, whether it's to return the enclosed reply card, call for an appointment for a tour, come to an open house, or whatever.

Make Your Grand Opening Truly Grand

Most family child-care center owners consider their business open when they get their license or when the first child arrives. For commercial centers, when the day comes for you to open your doors to youngsters for the first time, you'll probably feel a lot like a child yourself—an excited child about to open a pile of presents. What kind of day will it be? More important, what kind of day should it be?

In child care, there are two schools of thought on grand openings. One is to get as many people exposed to your business as quickly as you can with a splashy grand opening. The other is to not invest a great deal in a grand opening, because a year from now, it won't matter. For most child-care centers, the answer is somewhere in the middle.

Whether you decide to open with a bang or a whimper, the key to a successful opening is planning. Don't make this an impromptu party; it should be an integral part of your marketing strategy, carefully thought out and orchestrated for maximum results. Here are the key points you need to consider:

- *Budget*. Because your opening is a key element of your marketing plan, the cost of the event should come out of your marketing budget. Keep in mind that effective doesn't necessarily mean expensive, so don't go overboard with spending—and don't blow your entire first year's marketing budget on opening day. Think about what you want to accomplish and then think about what you can afford to accomplish. You might also ask suppliers and vendors to participate. Most will have promotional budgets of their own; they might have a display you can use or be willing to donate products such as food samples or other giveaway items. Remember, it's in their best interest to see you succeed.

> **Smart Tip** *Tip...*
>
> Ask every new client how they found out about you. Make a note of their answer and what kind of business they represent (how many children they could potentially refer to your business). This will let you know how well your various marketing efforts are working. You can then decide to increase certain programs and eliminate those that aren't working.

- *Type of event.* What sort of event will work for your grand opening? Should it be a party or a community or media event? Is it sufficient to use print advertising or direct mail to announce that you're open for business? The key is to make your opening event appropriate and appealing to your prospective customers.

  If you've decided to have a party or open house event, you might want to include local public officials on your guest list because they have a certain amount of celebrity stature in most communities. If they accept your invitation, be sure someone is available to play special host to them. Take care, however, to avoid giving your grand opening any inappropriate political overtones that may alienate prospective customers. Once you decide on the type of event, check with your local government to see if you need any special permits or licenses, and apply for them well in advance.

- *Timing.* There are a number of considerations when it comes to timing your opening ceremony. Should you hold your grand opening on your actual first day of business, or should you have what retailers call a "soft opening," where you actually operate your child-care center for a few days or weeks before you have a major celebration? There is some sound logic in not having your grand opening celebration on your actual opening day. You want everything to be working perfectly when you bring in special guests. You want to be sure everyone on your staff is prepared and that the facility is ready.

- *Time of day.* If you know that most of your customers are working during the day, you may think evening is the best time for an event. But if you're hoping to get media coverage, think again. Media representatives won't cover such mundane events as a small-business opening at night unless you have a major celebrity scheduled to appear.

- *Conflicting events.* Be careful that your opening doesn't conflict with another event that is targeting the same market or might in some way have a negative impact on you. For example, your market might not be sports fans, but a major sporting event could cause traffic problems and prevent customers from getting to your location. On the other hand, you might be able to piggyback on a national holiday or local celebration, so do some research and find out what will be going on. Any community booster group should be able to help you find out what's scheduled.

Plan Ahead

Allow adequate time to plan and prepare for your grand opening so that the event itself goes smoothly and creates the momentum your center will need. How long depends on your goals and the type of event, but it could be anywhere from a few weeks to a year. As soon as you set an opening date and decide what type of event you want, begin making lists of what needs to be done by when.

If you're going to be in a commercial location, put "Coming Soon" signs in the windows as soon as you lease or buy the space. Let your friends, family, suppliers, and other business associates know what you're doing. Prepare a media kit, build your contact list, and promote your new center every chance you get.

Media Kits That Get Results

A media kit is an essential tool if you want exposure in print, on television or radio, or even through internet sources. It will provide important information to reporters and establish your credibility. The basic elements of a good media kit include:

- *A one- or two-page fact sheet.* This provides a quick overview of the company in an easy-to-read format and typically includes information such as a description of your center and services, company history, key personnel, number of employees, number of offices and locations, statistical information (how many children you can serve, hours of operation), any other distinguishing features about the company, and a contact person who can be reached both during and after normal business hours.

- *Biographies of key individuals.* If possible, keep them to one page and focus on the information that is pertinent to the center.

- *Photograph(s).* You may include professional photos of your center, ideally showing children enjoying the facilities. You may also include headshots of you and your key staffers.

- *A news release.* Ideally, the release should be specific to the reporter's needs, or it may be about any timely or current event of interest to the reporter (as long as it relates to child care or children's transportation).

- *Cover letter.* This should either make reference to the fact that the kit was requested or, if you have not made prior contact, is pitching a specific story. Keep in mind that more is not always better; reporters don't have time to wade through pages of material looking for the information they need, so make sure everything you include in your kit has a reason for being there.

Finally, let your media kit work for you in other ways. You may use your kit as a tool to attract investors to fund expansion. You can also use it as a recruiting device for top employee

---

Bright Idea

Position yourself as a child-care expert with the local media. Let them know you are an easily accessible source whenever they need a comment on any aspect of child care, particularly if they are looking for a local angle to a national story.

talent, to support loan applications, or on any other occasion when you want to showcase your center in a positive way.

Referrals Are Essential

Referrals will likely be a primary way you get new clients, so it's a good idea to have a systematic approach to the process. You should be able to identify who is making referrals that ultimately turn into business so you can cultivate and reward those referral sources.

If a parent refers someone to one of Lois Mitten Rosenberry's centers and the child enrolls and stays for a month, the referring parent receives a $100 tuition credit. Janet Hale offers a $50 referral credit.

Bright Idea

One of the most effective ways to build your customer list is word-of-mouth. Provide superior service by taking excellent care of the children and making sure their parents know it, and you will increase the likelihood that they will spread the word about your business to other parents.

The Deal on Discounts

Should you offer corporate discounts? Some companies may ask you to give their employees a discount; the idea is that they are using your company to offer a benefit to their workers, and you are receiving some free advertising. Or you may find a landlord who will offer a concession on the rent in exchange for a discount on services for the landlord's employees. It can work, but be cautious.

Don't agree to any discounts until you are certain you understand your expenses and can be sure that a discount will not mean operating at a loss on a particular child or group of children. Then consider what you are getting in exchange and how difficult it would be to fill the discounted spaces with children paying the full rate. You may find you can stay full without offering discounts at all.

Mitten Rosenberry says she is routinely asked by companies to offer discounts and usually declines. "The fact is, it costs money to run a child-care center, and if you start to discount it, you are the one who will come up short. It's costing you every bit as much to provide child care for the employee who is getting the discount as it does for someone who isn't," she points out.

An alternative to giving discounts is to offer value-added services. For example, you may offer to speak to the company's employees on parenting issues or give their employees priority in terms of space availability.

Of course, if the company is offering you a substantial service, such as land or equipment, in exchange for a discount, you'll want to consider it. Run the numbers, and only do it if it can be a win-win situation.

Your Logo

Creating a logo for your child-care center that will appear on your business cards, letterhead, envelopes, contracts, sign, and company vehicle is an important part of developing your marketing package.

If you have sufficient artistic skills, you may want to create the logo yourself. Otherwise, hire a freelance designer or graphic artist to do this for you. Although the cost will vary depending on your geographical location, most freelance graphic artists will handle your job for $500 to $1,000 and provide you with camera-ready art and a digital file of your logo as well as your letterhead, business cards, and other materials.

Your Sign

Your child-care center's sign is the most important contact between your operation and much of the outside world. It is usually the first thing a potential client sees. It should be sufficiently bright and conspicuous to attract attention without being garish, and sufficiently informative so passersby immediately recognize what you do.

Drive around town and note which signs catch your eye in a positive manner and which ones don't. You'll want to consider what it was about signs you barely noticed— and signs you noticed but found unappealing. Remember that first impressions last and are hard to change.

Check your zoning requirements and/or the restrictions that may be placed on the property by the landlord, and then develop the basic design of your sign. It should include your logo and business name. Have it professionally made and installed so that it can be seen easily from all directions. Don't cut corners on this important advertising device. If your sign looks professional, potential clients are more likely to conclude that your center is a professional operation.

Going Online

Does your business need an internet presence? For a small homebased child-care operation, probably not. But for a commercial operation, yes. Although few people will make the final choice of a child-care provider or transportation service based on a web site, the fact is that many people look to the internet for resources and information. A web site can be a good marketing tool and a way for you to communicate with parents.

13

Staffing

This chapter discusses some of the staffing issues that are specific to child-care centers.

Gingerbread House owner Janet Hale says one of the most challenging parts of owning a child-care center is managing the staff. "Each teacher does [things] differently, but

I have a philosophy and a way of treating children that I want them to use," she says. "I want them to do it my way." And you'll likely want the same thing, which means you must hire smart and train right.

Your state will set a minimum child-to-staff ratio, and this should be taken as exactly that—a bare minimum. State regulations focus on the minimum requirements of child health and safety and offer very few stipulations about the educational or enrichment value of your programs.

The child-to-staff ratio is one of the factors that will strongly affect the type of center you run. If you are merely providing a facility to safely house children, minimum ratios of 10 or 15 children to every one adult will be sufficient. If you intend to market your center as an educational, enriching program that will offer more than institutionalized baby-sitting, you will have to lower the ratio to five or eight children to every one adult. This will, of course, cut into your profits, but a high-quality program will also justify offsetting additional expenses with higher rates. Further, if your center takes preschoolers and school-age children, you can rely on part-time workers in the after-school hours when your child occupancy will be highest. These are only general child-to-staff guidelines. Check your state's regulations for specifics on child-to-staff ratio requirements.

Ready, Set, Wait

Before you set up the first interview with an applicant, there are things you should do to make the hiring process go as smoothly as possible.

- ○ *Decide in advance what you need. You know you need help, but exactly what kind of help?* Do you need a caregiver or administrative support? In the very beginning, you'll be looking for people to do the tasks you can't or don't want to do. As you grow, you'll be looking for people who can help you expand your capabilities.

- ○ *Write job descriptions.* Take the time to put a list of responsibilities and required skills in writing. This forces you to think through what type of person will best meet your needs, which reduces the risk of hiring the wrong person. It also gives you something to show applicants so they are able to tell if the job you are offering is the one they want.

- ○ *Set basic personnel policies.* Don't think that because you're a small company you can just deal with personnel issues as they come up. You'll avoid a lot of problems down the road if you set policies in advance.

When to Hire

It's a good idea to hire people before you are in desperate need of them. Waiting until the last minute may drive you to make hiring mistakes, which can cost you dearly both in terms of cash and quality of care.

When you first begin hiring people, you may want to consider bringing them on as part-timers until your business grows to the point that full-timers are required. One of the biggest keys to getting and keeping good people is flex-ibility, and you'll find plenty of talented folks who for whatever reason don't want to work full time. If you can accommodate them, you'll both benefit. And as the workload grows and you need a full-time person doing that particular job, either change the status of your part-timer or, if that won't work, be creative: Consider hiring a second part-timer or setting up a job-sharing situation, or some other solution that will allow you to retain a valuable person and still get the work done.

Beware!
Before you hire your first employee, make sure you are prepared. Have all your paperwork ready, know what you need to do in the way of tax reporting, and understand all the liabilities and responsibilities that come with having employees.

Deciding What You Need

The first step in the prehiring phase is to decide exactly what you want someone to do. The job description doesn't have to be as formal as one you might expect from a large corporation, but it needs to clearly outline the person's duties and responsibilities, such as supervising children, coordinating games, implementing programs, preparing and/or serving lunches and snacks, changing diapers, etc. It should also list any special skills or other required credentials, such as a valid driver's license and clean driving record for someone who is going to be driving a company vehicle with children in it.

Next, you need to establish a pay scale. Ranges vary in different areas of the country, from about $5.75 per hour to $9 per hour, with the national average $8.47. For example, the average hourly wage for child-care workers in Connecticut is $9.79; in Massachusetts, it's $10.02; in California, it's $9.76; and in Arkansas, it's $6.74. You can get a good idea of the pay ranges in your area by checking the classified ads in your local newspaper.

For drivers, salaries can range from $300 to $450 a week (most driver jobs for children's transportation companies do not require a full 40-hour week) or $9 to $12 per hour. Paying drivers a salary rather than an hourly rate could make it easier for you to budget and encourages drivers to be more efficient. It also reduces the temptation for employees to be less than completely honest when filling out time sheets. Make the choice based on what seems to work best with the system you set up.

You'll also need a job application form. You can get a basic form at most office supply stores or you can create your own. In any case, have your attorney review the form you'll be using for compliance with the most current employment laws.

Every prospective employee should fill out an application—even if it's someone you know and even if they have submitted a detailed resume. A resume is not a signed, sworn statement acknowledging that you can fire a person if he or she lies; an application is. The application will also help you verify the person's resume; compare the two and make sure the information is consistent.

Now you're ready to start looking for candidates.

Where to Look for Candidates

Child-care center operators agree that one of their biggest challenges is staffing—finding and keeping qualified caregivers and assistants. Help-wanted ads are expensive and often don't produce much response. Be creative; network among people you know, put notices on bulletin boards in churches and community areas, check with school placement offices—in short, go to the candidates. Don't wait for them to come to you.

Lois Mitten Rosenberry finds employees for Children's Discovery Center through colleges, newspaper ads, job fairs, parent and staff referrals, and walk-in applicants. "We have a good reputation in the community, so we get a good number of walk-ins," she says.

Preschools and child-care centers usually cannot offer the salary and benefits certified schoolteachers can earn, but students working on their teaching credentials are often a good source of staff, particularly when you're searching for qualified part-timers.

Your current employees can be an excellent source of referrals for new employees. Consider developing a program to pay a bonus when a candidate referred by an employee is hired and stays on the job for a particular length of time, such as six months or a year.

Positions

Even in a large center, you'll have only a few different job classifications. They are:

- Director: In the beginning, this will likely be you, and your job description will be a simple "does just about everything." You are the key to success in your operation. You must hire, train, supervise, plan curriculum and scheduling, budget, make purchases, promote the business, set up the books, handle enrollment, solve problems, and be an all-around entrepreneur actively running the company you have started. At some point, however, you may need to hire a director to take over the day-to-day administration while you work on growing the business. You will need someone with both organizational ability and expertise in dealing with children and parents.

- Administrative staff: Your need for administrative staff will vary depending on the size of your center. As you grow, you may need a receptionist/telephone operator and perhaps a part- or full-time bookkeeper. As with the director,

Smart Tip

From the day they are hired, tell employees what they must do to get a raise without having to ask for it. Then follow up by increasing their pay rates when they've earned it.

in the beginning, you will likely handle most of these jobs yourself. Sometimes you'll find caregivers who can assist you with certain administrative tasks, but be careful that such duties don't distract them from their primary responsibilities.

- Caregivers: You may refer to the people you hire to actually care for the children as teachers, caregivers, aides, or assistants. State regulations will be the foundation for your own guidelines regarding what these individuals can do, how many children they can be responsible for at one time, and what their education and experience must be.

- Cook: If you are going to prepare and serve meals in your facility, you'll need a cook. If you're just serving lunch, you may be able to get by with a part-time cook, but if you want your center to grow to a substantial size, this job will likely need to be full time. Look for someone with institutional experience who can assist with meal planning and also be in charge of food purchasing, storage, preparation, and cleanup.

- Janitor/custodian: You'll need someone to handle indoor and outdoor cleanup, minor maintenance, and perhaps laundry. You can either outsource this to a service or hire someone on your staff to do the work. If your facility is such that you can provide an apartment or living space to a couple, you may be able to also get nighttime security in the arrangement. This type of arrangement could easily appeal to retirees on fixed incomes.

Evaluating Applicants

When you actually begin the hiring process, don't be surprised if you are as nervous at the prospect of interviewing potential employees as they are about being interviewed. After all, they may need a job, but the future of your company is at stake.

It's a good idea to prepare your interview questions in advance. Develop open-ended questions that encourage candidates to talk. In addition to knowing what they've done, you want to find out how they did it. Ask all candidates for a particular position the same set of questions, and take notes as they respond so you can make an accurate assessment and comparison later.

When the interview is over, let the candidate know what to expect. Is it going to take you several weeks to interview other candidates, check references, and make a decision? Will you want the top candidates to return for a second interview? Will you call the candidate, or should the person call you? This is not only a good business practice; it is also just simple common courtesy.

Always check with former employers and personal references. Though many companies are very restrictive as to what information they will verify, you may be surprised at what you can find out. You should at least confirm that the applicant told the truth about dates and positions held. Personal references are likely to give you some additional insight into the general character and personality of the candidate; this will help you decide if he or she will fit into your operation.

Keep in mind that under the Immigration Reform and Control Act of 1986, you may only hire persons who may legally work in the United States, which means citizens and nationals of the United States, and aliens authorized to work in the United States. As an employer, you must verify the identity and employment eligibility of everyone you hire. During the interviewing process, let the applicant know that you will be doing this. Once you have made the job offer and the person is brought on board, you must complete the Employment Eligibility Verification Form (I-9) and then retain it for at least three years, or one year after employment ends, whichever period of time is longer.

Be sure to document every step of the interview and reference-checking process. Even very small companies are finding themselves targets of employment discrimination suits; if it happens to you, good records are your best defense.

Caregiver Characteristics and Qualifications

The better qualified your staff is, the more attractive they and your service are to prospective customers. So what should you look for in the way of characteristics and qualifications? Specific education, certifications, and experience levels will likely be dictated by your state law. But in general, the caregivers you hire should have an understanding of child development and some training in early childhood education to make them sensitive and responsive to all the children in their care.

Stat Fact
Demographic projections indicate that finding good employees is going to be one of the biggest challenges all businesses face well into the 21st century.

Good caregivers know that learning occurs in informal activities as much as in formal instruction. They know that very young children have limited ability to communicate their wants and needs, and good caregivers are sensitive to each child's individual, developmental, and cultural characteristics.

The caregivers on your staff should be warm and loving and also have mature, healthful, positive attitudes about life, love, sex, and interpersonal relations. Remember that impressionable children pick up on the attitudes and behavior of the adults around them with amazing acuity.

Caregivers must be educated or instinctively adept at disciplining children fairly, without traumatizing them. They must have the skills to implement play and instructional activity for groups of disorganized, rambunctious, strong-willed youngsters.

"I look for someone with patience, a quiet voice, and some education," says Hale. "I want someone with a nice appearance who takes care of herself because if she takes care of herself, the chances are good she's going to take care of the children."

Ultimately, you must go with your gut feeling. Ask yourself, "Would I leave my child in this person's hands?" If your response is negative or uncertain, do not hire the candidate.

Background Checks

Screen potential caregivers very carefully; negligent employees, or workers temperamentally unsuited to working with children, can harm the children, damage your reputation, and bring lawsuits.

Ask all applicants whether they have abused children in any way in the past. Let them know you will be conducting a background check to verify all their answers. Though it is unlikely that many people will admit to a history of child abuse, it is possible that the attention you direct to the issue will discourage them from seeking employment in child care. You should never hire anyone who admits to a history of abusing children.

You should also ask prospective employees if they are sexually oriented to children and decline to hire anyone who answers in the affirmative. Because this can be a difficult and awkward conversation to have, include the question on your pre-employment form or job application. The question should read something like "Do you ever think you would like to have a sexual experience with a child?"

Don't try to conduct the background checks yourself. This is a task best left to an expert. Expect to pay anywhere from $50 to $200 for a professional background check, depending on how much detail you need. Check your telephone directory under "Investigative Services" to find a resource for background checks, or ask other business owners for a referral.

Let applicants know from the very beginning that you will be conducting such a check and

Bright Idea

Call local law firms and ask if they offer free newsletters on employment law or other issues that affect your operation. Most firms will be happy to add you to their mailing lists at no charge.

what you'll be looking for. Do this even for applicants you know and consider friends. Christine Srabian has several backup care providers, including her in-laws and neighbors, and all have gone through fingerprinting and a background check. Many will not even bother to fill out an application or take the time for an interview if they know they can't pass the background check.

Once They're on Board

The hiring process is only the beginning of the challenge of having employees. You need to provide a complete orientation for new employees.

Begin with a thorough tour of the facility. Even though you may have shown prospective employees around during the interviewing process, they should still receive an orientation tour that shows them everything in detail, from the reception area to the playground to where supplies are kept. You should also introduce them to other staff members. You might want to assign a "buddy" to new employees—someone they can go to with questions.

Your orientation and initial training should also include:

- Thorough discussion of the goals and philosophy of the facility, including some historical background of how it was formed and has grown
- The names and ages of the children for whom the caregiver will be responsible and their specific developmental needs
- Any special adaptation(s) of the facility required for a child with special needs
- Any special health or nutritional needs of the children assigned to the caregiver
- The planned program of activities at the facility
- Routines and transitions
- Acceptable methods of discipline
- Policies of the facility in regards to communicating with parents
- Meal patterns and food-handling policies
- Occupational health hazards for caregivers
- Emergency health and safety procedures
- Security policies and procedures
- General health policies and procedures, including hand-washing techniques; diapering techniques; toileting care; appropriate diaper disposal; food preparation, serving and storage techniques (if the employee will be preparing food); formula preparation (if formula is handled); child abuse detection, prevention and reporting; how to teach health promotion concepts to children and parents; and recognizing symptoms of illness

Oh, My Aching Back

Back injury is the most common cause of occupational injury for child-care providers. Instruct your caregivers that they can prevent back injury by using:

○ Proper lifting techniques, such as keeping the child as close as possible to you and avoiding any twisting motion as you lift the child; also, always lower the crib side before lifting the child out

○ Adult furniture; providers should not use child-sized chairs, tables, or desks

○ Adult-height changing tables

○ A ramp or small, stable stepladders or stairs to allow children, with constant supervision, to climb up to places to which they would ordinarily be lifted

○ Convenient equipment for moving children, reducing the necessity for carrying them long distances—for example, using a multiseat carriage to transport children to a nearby park

○ Comfortable chairs with back support (rockers, gliders, etc.) for holding children for long periods of time

A proper orientation ensures that all staff receive specific and basic training for the work they will be doing so they can carry out their responsibilities in a safe and effective manner.

Many small businesses conduct their "training" just by throwing someone into the job. That's not fair to the employee, and it's certainly not good for your business. If you think you can't afford to spend time training, think again—can you afford not to adequately train your employees? Do you really want them taking care of children without knowing exactly what to do?

In an ideal world, employees would be hired already knowing everything they need to know. But this isn't an ideal world, and if you want the job done right, you have to teach your people how to do it.

Whether done in a formal classroom setting or on the job, effective training begins with a clear goal and a plan for reaching it. Training falls into one of three major categories: orientation, which includes explaining company policies and procedures; job skills, which focuses on how to do specific tasks; and ongoing development, which enhances the basic job skills and grooms employees for future challenges and opportunities. These tips will help you maximize your training efforts:

- *Find out how people learn best.* Delivering training is not a one-size-fits-all proposition. People absorb and process information differently, and your training method needs to be compatible with their individual preferences. Some people can read a manual, others prefer a verbal explanation, and still others need to see a demonstration.

- *Be a strong role model.* Don't expect more from your employees than you are willing to do. You're a good role model when you do things the way they should be done all the time. Don't take shortcuts you don't want your employees to take or behave in any way you don't want them to behave.

> **Smart Tip** Tip...
>
> Even if you're starting a family child-care business and plan to be the only caregiver—and even though you may be very experienced at caring for children on an informal basis—professional child care is different. Your local Child Care Resource and Referral Agency or local Family Child Care Association can help with training resources for you and your staff.

On the other hand, don't assume that simply doing things the right way is enough to teach others how to do things. Role-modeling is not a substitute for training; it reinforces training. If you only role-model but never train, employees aren't likely to get the message.

- *Look for training opportunities.* Once you get beyond basic orientation and job skills training, you need to constantly be on the lookout for opportunities to enhance the skill and performance levels of your people.

- *Make it real.* Whenever possible, use real-life situations to train—but avoid letting the parents of the children in your care know they've become a training experience for employees.

- *Anticipate questions.* Don't assume that employees know what to ask. In a new situation, people often don't understand enough to formulate questions. Anticipate their questions and answer them in advance.

- *Ask for feedback.* Finally, encourage employees to let you know how you are doing as a trainer. Just as you evaluate their performance, convince them that it's OK to tell you the truth, ask them what they thought of the training and your techniques, and use that information to improve your own training skills.

Mitten Rosenberry says new employees at Children's Discovery Centers go through a two-hour orientation, and must then complete a training module on a CD-ROM before they begin working with children. Four additional training sessions must be completed within the following three to six months, covering issues such as curriculum, interaction with children, and classroom management.

Ongoing training is also a part of Mitten Rosenberry's policies. Teachers must attend an annual in-service training day; the centers are closed, and employees are paid for their time. Other training is provided throughout the year, and employees can take this training on their own time at no cost. Also, Mitten Rosenberry will consider reimbursing all or a portion of the costs to attend local, state, and national conferences, depending on where they are located and what is involved. Gingerbread House owner Janet Hale also pays for employees to attend conferences.

Temporary Employees

If your administrative, custodial, or kitchen staff needs a temporary increase (due to growth or employee absences), you can cover that need through a temporary help agency, which can be found in your telephone directory. It's a good idea to establish a relationship with one or two such agencies before you actually need them so you are comfortable that they will provide you with the staff you need. All temporary employees must meet the background check requirements (especially no record of child abuse of any kind) that regular employees meet.

Qualified temporary classroom help can be more difficult to find. When a caregiver calls in sick, your first source of assistance should be in-house. If you, as the director, are able to take that person's place, or if you can call in off-duty staff to cover, your problem is solved. If this is not possible, or if your temporary need is longer-term (such as when a caregiver suffers an extended illness or goes on vacation), you will need to find a qualified substitute.

Start by advertising in local newspapers for substitute teachers/caregivers and establish your own network. The same teachers who work as substitutes in preschools and kindergartens may also meet your state's requirements to work at your child-care facility. Credentialed schoolteachers who work as substitutes may be interested in being on your list for substitute work as well, particularly if you make the pay appealing.

Substitutes and temporary help of all kinds always command higher pay than regular staff because of a temporary help agency's additional costs and because the insecurity of performing temporary work needs to be offset by better wages.

If your advertising does not produce a sufficient pool of substitute candidates—say, one-third to one-half your staff size—contact your local school district and find out how to contact the pool of subs it relies on. Also, if many of your aides are students working on graduate

> **Bright Idea**
>
> Find out what your employees want in the way of benefits before you spend time and money developing a package. Do a brief survey. Ask what they think of the ideas you have, and ask them to come up with ideas of their own.
>
> If they want something you can't afford to do, don't reject it immediately. Figure out what you can afford and explain the situation to employees.

degrees in teaching, they may have classmates who are not interested in full-time work but would like some extra money on occasion. If they are qualified, give them a brief training session—paid, of course—and have them on standby for emergencies.

Employee Benefits

The wages you pay may be only part of your employees' total compensation. Although many very small companies do not offer a formal benefits program, more and more business owners have recognized that benefits—particularly in the area of insurance—are extremely important when it comes to attracting and retaining quality employees. In most parts of the country, the unemployment rate is lower than it's been in decades, which means competition for good people is stiff.

Bright Idea

If you have employees, consider using a payroll service rather than trying to handle this task yourself. The service will calculate taxes; handle reporting and paying local, state, and federal payroll taxes; make deductions for savings, insurance premiums, loan payments, etc.; and may offer other benefits to you and your employees.

Typical benefits packages include group insurance (your employees may pay all or a portion of their premiums), paid holidays, and vacations. Some services offer year-end bonuses based on the company's profitability. You can build employee loyalty by seeking additional benefits that may be somewhat unusual—and they do not have to cost much. For example, if you're in a commercial location, talk to store owners in your shopping center to see if they're interested in providing reciprocal employee discounts. You'll not only provide your own employees with a benefit, but you may get some new customers out of the arrangement.

One type of insurance may not be optional. In most states, if you have three or more employees, you are required by law to carry workers' compensation insurance. This coverage pays medical expenses and replaces a portion of the employee's wages if injury occurs on the job. Although the chances of such an injury are low in a child-care setting, even if you have only one or two employees, you may want to consider obtaining this coverage to protect both them and you in the event of an accident.

Details and requirements vary by state. Contact your state's insurance office or your own insurance agent for information so you can be sure to be in compliance.

Beyond tangible benefits, look for ways to provide positive working conditions. Consider flexible working hours, establish family-friendly policies, and be sure the physical environment is comfortable not only for the children but also for their caregivers. Hale points out that most child-care workers appreciate their schedules, particularly in centers that are open traditional hours. "They get paid holidays, they don't work on weekends, and we try to work around their family needs," she says.

The High Cost of Turnover

Employee turnover is a very important issue in the child-care industry, especially in caregiver positions. Low wages and high stress are both factors in the industry's high turnover rate. Whatever you can do to retain good employees will help your center tremendously.

Some of the costs of turnover are fairly easy to calculate; others are essentially priceless. When someone leaves, you have the hard costs of paying overtime to other employees to get that job done until a replacement is found, of recruiting (advertising, screening, interviewing, etc.), and of training. Those numbers are fairly easy to figure. Harder to calculate is the cost of making a hiring mistake. Also, there's the cost in customer relations and goodwill, and you may even lose a few customers who opt to follow the departed employee to a different child-care center.

A key to keeping employee turnover down is to avoid seeing your relationship as an employer-employee one, but rather as partners. That certainly includes bonuses and profit-sharing programs, but it goes beyond pure financial incentives. Employees need to participate in the decision-making process; they need to be encouraged to contribute ideas and solutions.

Beware!
Sometimes small companies lose good employees to larger firms that have better career opportunities. They may not be attracted as much by the money and benefits as they are by the room to grow and advance. Do the best you can to offer career growth to your people, but understand that it may not be enough to keep them there.

People also need to be treated with fairness and compassion. It isn't realistic to expect people to leave their personal lives at home. When an employee needs to take a few hours off to watch a child perform in a play or is dealing with an elderly parent requiring full-time nursing care, it's not only kind but wise for you to provide as much assistance as possible. Along with doing the humane thing, you'll be building a level of employee loyalty that can't be bought for any amount of salary.

Mitten Rosenberry says her turnover rate dropped when she increased wages and expanded her benefits package. "If we do something that decreases turnover, it saves us in training dollars and the parents are happier," she says. "You can't accurately measure all the costs of turnover, but our track record shows it's worth trying to keep it down." She also rewards employee performance with cash bonuses and merit salary increases. Because recognition is a strong motivator, Mitten Rosenberry names an employee of the month, using input from both co-workers and the children's parents, and sponsors an annual employee appreciation banquet.

Maintain Adequate Personnel Files

You should maintain current personnel records on all your employees. This should include a current photo (update it annually), which can be taken by you or another staff member with an instant camera in your office. If the person drives as part of the job, you should maintain a copy of a current, valid driver's license on file. Keep home addresses, telephone numbers, and emergency contact information current on all employees. Any special qualifications should be documented. Also, include certifications and documentation of any training completed after the employee joins your company.

Child-to-Staff Ratios

The child-to-staff ratio (the number of children for which each child-care provider is responsible) affects the quality of care a provider can give to each child. Small group sizes and low child-to-staff ratios are recommended by the American Public Health Association (APHA), the American Academy of Pediatrics (AAP), and the National Association for the Education of Young Children (NAEYC). Having a smaller number of infants/toddlers/children for each adult to take care of has been associated with:

- Children imitating earlier, and more often than usual, the speech and gestures of others
- Providers having more time to give the best care to children
- Children talking and playing more often
- Children being in distress less often
- Children being less exposed to danger

Grouping children in smaller numbers has also been associated with:

- Providers being able to give better attention to the children
- Children having more positive developmental outcomes
- Children being more cooperative and more responsive to adults and other children
- Children being more likely to speak without being prompted
- Children being less likely to wander aimlessly or be uninvolved in activities
- Children scoring higher on standardized tests

The following chart gives American Public Health Association/American Academy of Pediatrics recommendations by age for group size and child-to-staff ratios. Your state's regulations may be different.

Age	Maximum Group Size	Child-to-Staff Ratio
0 to 24 months	6	3:1
25 to 30 months	8	4:1
31 to 35 months	10	5:1
3 years	14	7:1
4 to 6 years	16	8:1

Maintaining your child-to-staff ratios when you offer full-day and partial-day care and have different age groups can be a challenge, especially for family child-care centers. It's possible for these homebased operations to have more children enrolled than can be at the center at the same time, so careful scheduling is essential.

Facility
Maintenance

The maintenance of a child-care center, whether homebased or in a commercial location, is a never-ending process. Lawns must be mowed, carpets vacuumed, and toilets scrubbed. These and other necessary tasks can be performed by a regular member of your staff, requiring you to purchase equipment and supplies to do the task, or they can be done by outside contractors.

Develop checklists (like the sample playground equipment list on page 159) that are appropriate for your operation so that you can be sure everything that needs to be done gets done and so you have records documenting maintenance and inspections in case you ever need them.

It's also critical that you stay current on product recalls so that you can immediately remove or repair anything in your facility that might be unsafe. For more information about recalls of children's toys and products—and to get recall notices sent directly to you by fax or e-mail—contact the U.S. Consumer Product Safety Commission (see Appendix).

Building Maintenance

Develop a cleaning schedule and assign tasks to the appropriate staff member. If you use an outside cleaning or janitorial service, a staff member should still check to make sure the work has been completed satisfactorily.

Porches, steps, stairs, and walkways should be kept free from accumulations of water, ice, and snow and should be in overall good repair. Guardrails and banisters should be checked regularly to be sure they are securely attached to the wall or floor and have not been pulled loose by use. Storage areas should be kept clean and in good order.

Your local building or fire inspector can advise you of proper procedures for maintaining furnace and boiler equipment.

Periodically check windows, exterior doors, and basement or cellar hatchways to be sure they are in sound condition and tightly sealed. Children's environments must be protected from exposure to moisture, dust, and excessive temperatures.

Check electrical fixtures and outlets to be sure they are properly functioning. Of course, any outlets not in use should be securely covered.

Humidifiers, dehumidifiers and air-handling equipment that involves water should be cleaned and disinfected at least once a week.

Exterior Maintenance

In the case of grounds maintenance, if you have a commercial center, you will probably want to hire a lawn care service. The cost of buying a lawn mower, edger, rakes, hedge clippers, and large trash cans—or the hassle of bringing your own from home every week or two—will be prohibitive. Shop around for a service that offers competitive rates, is bonded and insured, and comes recommended by other business owners.

Be sure your lawn care service is careful with the use of chemicals and only uses chemicals according to manufacturers' instructions and in a manner that will not contaminate play surfaces or articles. The Environmental Protection Agency in Washington, DC (see Appendix), will provide you with a list of restricted chemicals that are not suitable for use in a child-care environment.

Regardless of who is doing the work, be sure outside walkways are kept free of loose objects and in good repair. All outdoor areas should be kept free of excessive dust, weeds, brush, high grass, and standing water.

Janitorial needs are also best handled by a service rather than by someone on staff. It is unlikely you will find a qualified child-care worker who is also willing to clean floors and restrooms after a long day of minding small children. As with lawn care services, shop around for a janitorial service that offers competitive rates, is bonded and insured, and comes recommended by other business owners. You'll find both of these types of businesses listed in your local telephone directory.

Of course, you'll want to have some cleaning supplies and some equipment on hand to deal with the spills and messes a group of small children will inevitably produce. A broom and dustpan will cost only a few dollars. Sufficient towels, cleaning rags, and supplies will cost less than $50.

Assuming you hire lawn care and janitorial services, you should still have the following equipment on hand for occasional cleaning needs (quantities will vary depending on the size of your center):

- 4 19-gallon litter receptacles
- 10 wastebaskets
- 1 mop pail and press
- 1 mop handle
- 2 mop heads
- 1 push broom
- 2 dustpans
- 1 mobile litter receptacle

If you don't hire lawn care and janitorial services, you'll also need the following:

- 1 vacuum cleaner

Bright Idea

Invite parents to help with some maintenance and special projects. "We sometimes ask the parents to come down and help us haul sand," says Janet Hale, owner of Gingerbread House in Exeter, California. "A lot of the sand we keep under the playground equipment goes home in the kids' shoes, and we have to replace it periodically." Parents are usually happy to help and enjoy being involved in the center's activities.

▲

- 1 floor polisher
- 2 garden hoses
- 1 power lawn mower
- 1 power edger

Equipment Maintenance

Even the highest-quality equipment can wear out, especially when used on a daily basis by rambunctious youngsters. Periodic monitoring ensures that hazards are either removed or corrected.

The playground equipment should be checked on a monthly basis. Use the checklist below, maintaining records of your inspections in your files. Also, use the "Safety Checklist" on page 160 to give your facility an overall checkup.

Playground Equipment Checklist

Equipment name/identifier_____

- ❑ Visible cracks, bending, warping, rusting, or breakage
- ❑ Deformation of open hooks, shackles, rings, links, etc.
- ❑ Worn swing hangers and chains
- ❑ Missing, damaged, or loose swing seats
- ❑ Broken supports or anchors
- ❑ Cement support footings that are exposed, cracked, or loose in the ground
- ❑ Accessible sharp edges or points
- ❑ Exposed ends of tubing that require covering with plugs or caps
- ❑ Protruding bolt ends that have lost caps or covers
- ❑ Loose bolts, nuts, etc., that require tightening
- ❑ Splintered, cracked, or otherwise deteriorating wood
- ❑ Lack of lubrication on moving parts
- ❑ Worn bearings or other mechanical parts
- ❑ Broken or missing rails, steps, rungs, or seats
- ❑ Worn or scattered surfacing material
- ❑ Hard surfaces, especially under swings, slides, etc. (places where resilient material has been shifted away from any surface underneath play equipment)
- ❑ Chipped or peeling paint
- ❑ Pinch or crush points, exposed mechanisms, juncture, and moving components

Problems found: _____

Corrective action taken: _____

Signature _____   Date _____

Safety Checklist

Here are some helpful guidelines for parents and child-care providers from the U.S. Consumer Product Safety Commission.

❑ *Cribs.* Make sure cribs meet current national safety standards and are in good condition. Look for a certification safety seal. Older cribs may not meet current standards. Crib slats should be no more than $2\frac{3}{8}$ inches apart, and mattresses should fit snugly. This can prevent strangulation and suffocation associated with older cribs and mattresses that are too small.

❑ *Soft bedding.* Be sure that no pillows, soft bedding, or comforters are used when you put babies to sleep. Babies should be put to sleep on their backs in a crib with a firm, flat mattress. This can help reduce Sudden Infant Death Syndrome and suffocation related to soft bedding.

❑ *Playground surfacing.* Look for safe surfacing on outdoor playgrounds—at least 12 inches deep of wood chips, mulch, sand, or pea gravel, or mats made of safety-tested rubber or rubberlike materials. This helps protect against injuries from falls, especially head injuries.

❑ *Playground maintenance.* Check playground surfacing and equipment regularly to make sure they are maintained in good condition. This can help prevent injuries, especially from falls.

❑ *Safety gates.* Be sure that safety gates are used to keep children away from potentially dangerous areas, especially stairs. Safety gates can protect against many hazards, especially falls.

❑ *Window blind and curtain cords.* Be sure mini-blinds and Venetian blinds do not have looped cords. Check that vertical blinds, continuous looped blinds, and drapery cords have tension or tie-down devices to hold the cords tight. These safety devices can prevent strangulation in the loops of window blind and curtain cords.

❑ *Clothing drawstrings.* Be sure there are no drawstrings around the hood and neck of children's outerwear clothing. Other types of clothing fasteners—like snaps, zippers, hook-and-loop fasteners, or Velcro—should be used. Drawstrings can catch on playground and other equipment and can strangle young children.

❑ *Recalled products.* Make sure no recalled products are being used and that a current list of recalled children's products is readily visible. Recalled products pose a threat of injury or death. Displaying a list of recalled products will remind caretakers and parents to remove or repair potentially dangerous children's toys and products.

When Things Go Wrong

Children are the most vulnerable members of our society, and child-care providers have a tremendous responsibility for their safety and well-being. The list of what could go wrong in a child-care center ranges from a minor bump or bruise to a death and includes thousands of possibilities in between.

▲

The first step in dealing with problems is to be proactive and put together systems to prevent them from happening in the first place.

Security

The reality of the world in which we live makes tight security in child-care facilities critical. Although shootings and hostage situations in centers make the headlines when they happen, they are still relatively rare. Even so, child-care centers are frequently the scenes of crimes, including domestic abuse, custody disputes, and other occurrences that create tense emotional situations that can physically or mentally harm a child.

A particular challenge that child-care operators face is reconciling the need for an open environment where parents are encouraged to visit with the need for tight security measures to protect the children. Use these tips to add a measure of security to your facility while still maintaining a warm, friendly atmosphere:

- *Have a gatekeeper.* This is the person—usually the center's receptionist/secretary—in charge of screening outsiders and acting as a buffer between the classrooms and the outside world. This individual should be trained to deal with security issues such as knowing who to call for information or security backup and how to keep unwanted visitors out of classrooms. This person should also be kept updated on any custodial or domestic situations involving staff members and/or children and be given the means to deal with those situations appropriately and effectively.

- *Consider hiring security personnel for high-hazard times.* Evening pickup is the most common time for altercations between adults, especially those involving custody situations. The presence of a trained, uniformed security officer can be an effective deterrent to crimes against staff and children and can be of great assistance after hours. To afford such help, consider asking your parents and staff to contribute to a security fund—many parents will be willing to help if you tell them why you want to hire an officer.

- *Be proactive about high-risk situations.* At the beginning of each year, send a request asking to be notified of any change in domestic status for children and staff, stating that this request is done for security purposes only. Share this information discreetly and on a need-to-know basis with staff members.

> **Bright Idea**
> Update your emergency information and contact form at least twice a year. Ask the parents to review what you have on file and either date and initial the form if it is still accurate, or update it if it is not. Use this to reinforce the fact that you are providing a safe place for their child.

- *Provide each classroom with some form of communication with the main office and outside world.* Too often, caregivers are isolated in classrooms where they have no means of getting help in an emergency. Intercoms, walkie-talkies, handheld radios, and cell phones are all options to consider.

- *Consider a metal detector for larger facilities.* Though it may be considered an extreme measure, metal detectors can be an effective deterrent against concealed weapons, especially if you have a large number of visitors to your center. It sends a message that you are not an easy target.

- *Have floor plans of your facility available both on- and off-site.* Physical descriptions of your building and rooms are useful in the event of any emergency and make the jobs of law enforcement and rescue personnel much easier. The plans should indicate features such as windows, doors, water shut-off valves, and electrical breaker boxes. They should also note the location of any communication devices such as televisions, telephones, and computers.

- *Train staff to deal with violent situations.* Staff members should know how to proceed in various situations when they are confronted with angry people.

- *Maintain copies of emergency contact information off-site.* In emergency situations, names and phone numbers of parents, children, and caregivers become critical. Who is in and out of the building is also important information that should be available from a secure location in case the office is not accessible for any reason.

At Lois Mitten Rosenberry's Toledo, Ohio, child-care centers, each building is protected by an entry system; parents are assigned a code that allows them to enter the building. Parents are also issued a "green card," which allows them—or anyone they designate—to pick up their child. (Turn to page 164 to see the green card.) The names of people authorized to pick up a particular child are kept on file, and that person must also present a green card before the child will be released.

Also, Mitten Rosenberry has trained her caregivers that when they are outside with the children, they should always be on the alert for problems. "We ask our employees not to congregate on the playground," she explains. "They are not to stand out there talking with each other but are to position themselves around the playground. If they see anyone suspicious, they are to immediately take the children inside. And that has happened a few times. For example, once a drunk tried to get on a playground. Our staff knew what to look for, and they took the children inside, locked the doors, and called the police."

Smart Tip *Tip...*

Have emergency numbers (911, police, ambulance, and poison control center) posted by every phone. For less critical situations, have the number for "Ask A Nurse" (a common name for free telephone information services offered by local hospitals in most communities) or a similar medical reference source handy.

Green Card

CHILDREN'S DISCOVERY CENTER

I, the undersigned,
may pick up

_____

from Children's Discovery Center.

Signature: _____

Relationship to Child: _____

Security is no less critical in a family child-care setting. Suzanne Wright, who runs a homebased child-care business in Ellicott City, Maryland, says, "I am very safety-conscious. It is my number-one priority for the children. I keep my doors locked throughout the day, provide only age-appropriate toys, feed only acceptable food that I consider not to be a choking hazard, and keep my dog separate from the kids." Be sure the children you care for know they are not allowed to open the door, and never open the door yourself to someone you don't know.

Preventing and Dealing with Injuries

When it comes to preventing and dealing with injuries, nothing replaces good judgment. Beyond that, this section discusses some practical ways to reduce or eliminate injuries at your center and what to do when an incident occurs.

The risk of an injury happening is directly related to the physical environment and children's behaviors, and how these are managed. Injuries can be divided into two categories—unintentional and intentional. Unintentional injuries may result from choking, falls, burns, drowning, swallowing toxic or other materials (poisoning), cuts, exposure to environmental hazards (such as chemicals, radon or lead), animal bites, or other accidents. Intentional injuries are usually due to bites, fights, or abuse.

You can prevent most injuries that occur in the child-care setting by:

- Supervising children carefully
- Checking the child-care and play areas for, and getting rid of, hazards
- Using safety equipment for children, such as car seats and seat belts, bicycle helmets, and padding, such as for the knees and elbows

- Understanding what children can do at different stages of development. Children learn by testing their abilities. They should be allowed to participate in activities appropriate for their development even though these activities may result in some minor injuries, such as scrapes and bruises. However, children should be prevented from taking part in activities or using equipment that is beyond their abilities and that may result in major injuries, such as broken bones.
- Teaching children how to use playground equipment safely (e.g., going down the slide feet first)

One of Mitten Rosenberry's centers is located near an expressway exit ramp. At about 6 P.M. one evening, the brakes on a large dump truck failed, and the truck crossed four lanes of traffic and the child-care center's parking lot, and tore through the playground until it was stopped by a tree. Thankfully, no one was hurt; the children had all either gone home for the day or were inside waiting to be picked up. Mitten Rosenberry immediately installed a heavy-duty guardrail—at her own expense, because the city would not do it. Her advice: Look at traffic patterns around your center and install reinforced barricades if there's a risk that an out-of-control vehicle could end up in your playground or an area where children might gather.

When an injury does occur, it requires immediate action. You will need to assess the injury to determine what type of medical attention, if any, is required. Everyone working with children should have up-to-date training in first aid and cardiopulmonary resuscitation (CPR). At a minimum, one person with this training must be present at the child-care site at all times. If the injury is serious, call 911 or your local emergency number. Administer any other appropriate first aid or medical treatment and notify the parent. (See page 170 for a sample "Emergency Information and Contact Form" and page 166 for a sample consent form.) Record all injuries on a standard form developed for that purpose. (Turn to page 171 for a sample "Injury Report Form.")

Expect that injuries will occur, no matter how careful you are. That's why you need first-aid kits, training, reporting procedures, etc. You should have information on each child's medical care providers, such as the doctor, dentist and the hospital the parents prefer. There may be times when a trip to the emergency room is not necessary, but you may be asked to take the child to a doctor. Or the child may be taken to the emergency room, and the medical staff there finds that a consultation with the patient's primary care physician would be helpful. Maintain that information on a form similar to the one on page 170.

Though most parents are reasonable and understanding if their child suffers a minor injury during the day, some will not be. One owner we talked to shared the story of a youngster who got a minor cut, and when the mother came to pick up the child and take her to the doctor, she said, "I'm going to sue. I'm an attorney, I know how these things work, and I'm going to get some money out of this for my child's college education." That's where your insurance coverage (see Chapter 4) comes in.

▲

Parent/Guardian Consent and Agreement for Emergencies

As parent/guardian, I consent to have my child receive first aid by facility staff and, if necessary, be transported to receive emergency care. I will be responsible for all charges not covered by insurance. I give consent for the emergency contact person listed below to act on my behalf until I am available. I agree to review and update this information whenever a change occurs and at least every six months.

Parent/guardian signature _____

Date_____

Parent/guardian signature _____

Date_____

Emergency contact person: _____

Address: _____

Telephone: _____

Evacuation Plans

Each child-care facility should have a written plan for evacuation in the event of fire, and it should be posted in a visible area. You should also write up procedures for a chemical emergency (spill or accidental release). Each facility, as appropriate for its geographic area, should also have an evacuation plan for blizzard, earthquake, flood, hurricane, tornado, power failure, or other disasters that could create structural damages to the facility or pose health hazards. You should practice drills for fire (and for tornadoes in areas where they occur) every month. Drills for hurricanes and earthquakes should be practiced every six months in areas in which they are likely to occur. Keep a record of your practice drills.

Christine Srabian in Maryland routinely conducts fire drills. She says her smoke alarm often goes off when she's cooking ("not because of my cooking skills, but because it's in a really stupid place in my house," she insists), so the children are familiar with the sound. When the alarm goes off, she talks to the children about what they would do if the alarm were real. "We have a huge green utility box outside the house, and they know just to walk outside, sit on the utility box and don't move."

When You Suspect Abuse

Child-care providers are required by law to report abuse when they see evidence or have reasonable suspicions that a child is being mistreated. Each state defines abuse in its statutes, and while those definitions differ somewhat, most contain the following elements:

Smart Tip

A growing number of government agencies publish sex offender registries online. To find out if an online database is available for your community, call your local law enforcement agency. Or do an internet search for links to sex offender registry sites around the country.

- *Emotional abuse.* This consists of acts that damage a child in psychological ways but do not fall into other categories of abuse. For prosecution, most states require that psychological damage be very definite and clearly diagnosed by a psychologist or psychiatrist; this category of abuse is rarely reported and even more rarely a cause of protective action.
- *Neglect.* General neglect is a failure to provide the common necessities, including food, shelter, a safe environment, education, and health care, but without resultant or likely harm to the child. Severe neglect is neglect that results or is likely to result in harm to the child.
- *Physical abuse.* This is an intentional (nonaccidental) act affecting a child that produces tangible physical harm.
- *Sexual abuse.* This is any sexual act performed with a child by an adult or by another child who exerts control over the victim. (Many state laws provide considerable detail about the specific acts that constitute sexual abuse.)

Your licensing agency will instruct you on the steps to take when you suspect abuse. Whether or not it is required, you may want to take photographs for your own files of any injuries that may be the result of abuse.

Bicycle Safety

Bicycles can be lots of fun—and extremely dangerous. If you provide care for older children and permit bicycling as an activity, you should plan and use bike routes that have been reviewed and approved by your local police department. All children and adults should wear approved safety helmets while riding and should follow all applicable traffic regulations and safety procedures. This also applies to school-age children who use bicycles to travel from school to your facility. Young children who may not be able to identify and adjust to dangerous traffic situations should never be allowed to ride in the street unsupervised.

These tips can be used as the basis for your bicycle safety training:

- Always wear a helmet that is properly fitted, brightly colored for increased visibility, and does not interfere with vision or hearing.
- Before each ride, check the bicycle to make sure all parts are secure and working. Check the brakes to be sure they are properly functioning. Also, check the wheels before every ride, after a fall, and after the bicycle has been transported.
- Know your bike's capabilities, and be sure it is the right size for you.
- Wear clothes that make you visible to motorists.
- Make sure the bicycle has the right safety equipment: a red rear reflector, a white front reflector, a red or colorless spoke reflector on the rear wheel, an amber or colorless reflector on the front wheel, pedal reflectors, a horn or bell, and a rearview mirror. A bright headlight is recommended for night riding.
- Avoid bicycling at night, at dusk or dawn, or at times when visibility is poor.
- Stay alert at all times. Constantly watch for anything that could make you fall, such as opening car doors, sewer gratings, soft shoulders, broken glass, and other debris. Remember to keep a safe distance from the vehicle ahead. Be especially careful on wet streets or when there could be ice or frost on your path.
- Ride single-file in the same direction as other vehicles, on the right side of the road in a straight, predictable path.
- Check for traffic. Always look left, right, left, and then walk your bicycle into the street before mounting and beginning your ride. If already in the street, always look behind you for a break in traffic. Then signal before making a turn in any direction.
- Obey all traffic laws, signs, and signals. Cyclists must follow the same rules as motorists.
- Be courteous to pedestrians and other vehicle operators.
- Never hitch on cars. A sudden stop or turn could send you flying into the path of a vehicle.
- Carry no passengers (except in approved baby seats).

Reacting to a Crisis

No matter how well you prepare, there will be situations beyond your control and problems you can't avoid. You will need plans—such as the evacuation procedures discussed earlier—in place to deal with problems.

A key element of your plan should be what to do if a crisis occurs and the media get involved. Situations could include violence at your center, injuries to the children, or any situation where you and your business are inadvertently thrust into the spotlight.

Designate one individual as the company spokesperson. Everyone on your staff should know who that is and be taught to refer any media inquiries to that person. Your spokesperson should have some experience dealing with the media and should know how to answer questions without creating legal liability.

Mitten Rosenberry had a situation where a baby was bitten by another child. The center staff members were not at fault; the biting child was being dropped off and was still under the

> **Tip...**
>
> ## Smart Tip
>
> If you have a family child-care center, have a backup for yourself in case of an emergency. Suzanne Wright's husband is her backup care provider. Christine Srabian's mother-in-law, who lives in a basement apartment in Srabian's home, is her designated substitute; she also has several friends in the neighborhood who have passed background checks and step in to care for the children if necessary.

supervision of a grandparent when the incident occurred. But the baby's mother was upset and contacted a local television station, which filmed the outside of the center and the baby. On the advice of her attorney, Mitten Rosenberry refused to comment—but that, she realized later, was a mistake. Had she spoken to a reporter, she could have corrected some of the erroneous information that was broadcast. Also, her silence may have protected her in the event of a lawsuit, but it made her look guilty in the "court of public opinion." From that, she learned to turn to her attorney for legal advice and a public relations expert for public relations advice. So she sat down with a public relations firm and developed a crisis PR plan.

Emergency Information and Contact Form

Child's name: _____ Birthdate: _____

Parent/guardian #1 name: _____

Telephone: Home_____ Work_____

Pager/Car _____

Parent/guardian #2 name: _____

Telephone: Home_____ Work_____

Pager/Car _____

EMERGENCY CONTACTS
(to whom child may be released if guardian is unavailable)

Name #1:_____ Relationship_____

Telephone: Home_____ Work_____

Pager/Car _____

Name #2:_____ Relationship_____

Telephone: Home_____ Work_____

Pager/Car _____

CHILD'S PREFERRED SOURCES OF MEDICAL CARE

Physician's name _____

Address:_____ Telephone:_____

Dentist's name: _____

Address:_____ Telephone:_____

Hospital name: _____

Address:_____ Telephone:_____

Ambulance service: _____

Address:_____ Telephone:_____

(Parents are responsible for all emergency transportation charges.)

CHILD'S HEALTH INSURANCE

Insurance plan: _____

ID #:_____ Group #_____

Subscriber's name (on insurance card): _____

SPECIAL CONDITIONS, DISABILITIES,
ALLERGIES, OR MEDICAL EMERGENCY INFORMATION

_____

_____

Injury Report Form

ABC Child Care
111 Development Way
Peoria, IL 01234

Date of injury: _____

Time of injury: _____ ____A.M. ____P.M.

Name of Injured: _____

　　　Sex: __Male __Female

　　　Age: ___ years

Where injury happened: _____

_____

How injury happened: _____

_____

Part(s) of body injured: _____

_____

Objects involved (if any): _____

_____

What was done to help the injured: _____

_____

Parent/guardian advised:

　　　of injury: ___yes ___no

　　　to seek medical attention: ___yes ___no

Supervisor (at time of injury): _____

Person completing form: _____

Date form completed: _____

Tales from the Trenches

By now, you should know how to get started and have a good idea of what to do—and not do—in your own business. But nothing teaches as well as the voice of experience. We asked established operators to tell us what has contributed to their success; here's what they had to say.

▲

Invest in Yourself

You are your own greatest asset, and you should cultivate your own skills through training, professional development, and personal growth.

"I knew no one else had as much invested in this company as I did, so I decided that I would invest in me," Toledo, Ohio, child-care provider Lois Mitten Rosenberry says. From the very beginning, even when money was extremely tight, she included child-care and business conferences in her budget. "It has opened up a lot of opportunities to me," she says. "It has made me a better person and enabled me to take the company to where it is today."

In addition to training, join professional associations; most communities have an association of child-care providers, along with a wide range of organizations designed to support small-business owners.

Reach Out to the Community for Enrichment

No matter what size your center is, take advantage of the resources in your community to enrich your programs. For example, Mitten Rosenberry has an agreement with Toledo's Center of Science and Industry. "We pay one price, and the preschoolers can go there once a week and use the children's museum," she says.

Find out if your local police and fire departments will visit your facility and make presentations to the youngsters. It's a good idea to let the children see firefighters in full gear so they aren't afraid of them if an emergency occurs.

Find Out How You're Doing

Mitten Rosenberry asks parents to evaluate her centers and the care their children are receiving and uses that input when developing improvement plans. She also uses secret shoppers to find out not only how her own centers are doing, but how they compare with other centers. Occasionally, she brings in national consultants to analyze her performance and provide constructive feedback.

Differentiate Your Service

Position yourself in the marketplace as a child-care center that is unique. Mitten Rosenberry was concerned when a large chain moved into her community. But one of her advisors told her not to see competition as a negative, but rather to use it as a positive. "Learn to create a business that is so different from your competitors that the parents of the children will always choose you," she says. As she adopted unusual and innovative concepts in her centers, she began attracting attention.

"In differentiating my product, we received a lot of exposure on television and in the newspapers," she says. She won a number of awards in the general business community as well as the child-care industry, and each award generated more news coverage. "For as small of a company as we are, people are amazed at the publicity we have received," Mitten Rosenberry says. "But it comes from finding that niche, that way to do your product differently that gives you an edge in the marketplace."

One of the ways Mitten Rosenberry differentiates her centers is in how calls are handled when people are looking for information. As the first conversation begins, a record is created, tracking the caller's name, the name and age of the child (or children), what the parent is looking for in the way of child-care services, and any other information that is discussed. When the parent comes in to tour the facility, the administrator makes it a point to refer to the child by name and is able to focus on the aspects of the center that are consistent with what the parent wants.

Earn and Demand Respect

You are not "just a baby-sitter"—you are a professional with a tremendous amount of responsibility. "It takes a lot of either intuitive understanding of children, education, and/or experience to be a really good provider," says Ellicott City, Maryland, child-care operator Suzanne Wright. "It's not a career for someone just because they are not qualified to do something else. Raising someone else's children for more hours than are spent awake at their own home is a responsibility that should not be entered into without considerable thought."

Get Commitments from Your Customers

You make a long-term commitment to your business, so it's reasonable to expect your customers to make a commitment to using your services. Don't be afraid to ask your customers to sign a contract obligating them to use your services for a specified period of time. The contract can include an escape clause that lets either you or the customer out of the agreement under certain circumstances, but a contract tells your customers you are committed to them and their children, and you deserve the same in return.

Follow Up on Everything You Do

Take the time to study the impact of all the management and marketing things you do. When you make a management change, review the effect it has on your operation. And only do as much marketing as you have time to follow up on. For example, don't do a direct-mail campaign if you're not going to have time to answer the calls it generates. Don't ask for referrals if you're not going to follow up on them. If you exchange business cards with someone, always call them within a few days to see if they have any interest in your services.

Keep a Professional Distance

When you spend as much time with children as child-care providers do, it's easy to develop strong feelings for them. But keep those feelings under control. "You may love the kids and the parents, but you need to keep a professional distance," says Janet Hale, owner of Gingerbread House in Exeter, California. "Children will come and go, things happen in families, and while you want to be there to support the family, you can't let them devastate you."

"I'm surprised at how attached you get to these little people," says Christine Srabian. "You don't want to see them go when they grow up."

Keep in mind that you are essentially an extended family for the children, and they are likely to be very candid and open about what's going on at home. You're going to hear things that shouldn't be repeated. "Keep everything you know about the kids confidential," says Hale. "We hear lots of stuff—that daddy hit mommy, that grandpa left grandma for a younger woman. If kids are comfortable and love their teachers, and most of them do, they will say what's on their mind. And that could be that daddy left town or is in jail." Don't repeat anything the children say about their home lives, and routinely reinforce this in staff training sessions.

Be Prepared for the Bad Days

Having a child-care center isn't perpetual recess—it's long hours, hard work, and plenty of stress. Know that you'll have "those moments," when things are going wrong, the children are being difficult, and you're on your last nerve. At those times, take a moment to reflect and remind yourself why you started your business.

Enjoy the Rewards

Child-care providers say no other business can match theirs for personal satisfaction and emotional rewards.

"Even though we try to keep a professional distance, we become involved with the family over time," says Hale. "It warms my heart to see single mothers or struggling families make it, get good jobs, and get off public assistance."

There's also the tremendous gratification of watching children grow and develop physically, socially, and intellectually, and to know that you are playing a very important role in shaping the future of each child in your care. Beyond that important long-term benefit, there are the minute-by-minute rewards of being a child-care provider. After all, what can equal the warmth of a child's hug or the joy of their laughter?

Appendix
Child-Care Service Resources

They say that you can never be too rich or too thin. While we could argue with those premises, we do believe you can never have too many resources. Therefore, we present you with a wealth of sources to check into, check out, and harness for your own personal information blitz.

These sources are tidbits; ideas to get you started on your own research. They are by no means the only sources out there and should not be taken as the ultimate answer. We have done our research, but businesses tend to move, change, fold, and expand rapidly. As we have repeatedly stressed, do your homework. Get out and start investigating.

Associations

American Academy of Pediatrics (AAP), 141 N.W. Point Blvd., Elk Grove Village, IL 60007-1098, (847) 434-4000, fax: (847) 434-8000, www.aap.org

ASTM International (formerly *American Society for Testing and Materials*), 100 Barr Harbor Dr., West Conshohocken, PA 19428-2959, (610) 832-9585, fax: (610) 832-9555, www.astm.org

Center for the Child Care Workforce, 555 New Jersey Ave. NW, Washington, DC 20001, (202) 662-8005, fax: (202) 662-8006, www.ccw.org

Child Care Law Center, 221 Pine St., 3rd Fl., San Francisco, CA 94104, (415) 394-7144, fax: (415) 394-7140, www.childcarelaw.org

Children's Foundation, 725 15th St. NW, #505, Washington, DC 20005-2109, (202) 347-3300, fax: (202) 347-3382, www.childrensfoundation.net

National Association for Family Child Care, 5202 Pinemont Dr., Salt Lake City, UT 84123, (801) 269-9338, fax: (801) 268-9507, www.nafcc.org

National Association of Child Care Professionals, P.O. Box 90723, Austin, TX 78709, (800) 537-1118, fax: (512) 301-5080, www.naccp.org

National Child Care Association, 1016 Rosser St., Conyers, GA 30012, (800) 543-7161, fax: (770) 388-7772, www.nccanet.org

National Child Care Information Center, 10530 Rosehaven St., #400, Fairfax, VA 22030, (800) 616-2242, fax: (800) 716-2242, www.nccic.org

National Resource Center for Health and Safety in Child Care, University of Colorado Health Sciences Center in Denver, Campus Mail Stop F541, P.O. Box 6508, Aurora, CO 80045-0508, (800) 598-5437, fax: (303) 724-0960, www.nrc.uchsc.edu

Urban Institute, nonprofit policy research organization, 2100 M St. NW, Washington, DC 20037, (202) 833-7200, www.urban.org

Books and Publications

Better Baby Care: A Book for Family Day Care Providers, The Children's Foundation

Child Care Information Exchange, P.O. Box 3249, Redmond, WA 98073-3249, (800) 221-2864, www.ccie.com

Early Childhood News, 2 Lower Ragsdale, #125, Monterey, CA 93940, (831) 333-5500, www.earlychildhood.com

Early Childhood Today, Scholastic Inc., 557 Broadway, New York, NY 10012, (800) 724-6527, (303) 604-1464, www.scholastic.com

Helping Children Love Themselves and Others: A Professional Handbook for Family Day Care, S. Gellert, K. Hollestelle, and E. Kotlus, The Children's Foundation

High/Scope Educational Research Foundation, 600 N. River St., Ypsilanti, MI 48198-2898, (734) 485-2000, fax: (734) 485-0704, www.highscope.org

Safe Ride News Publications, P.O. Box 77327, Seattle, WA 98177-0327, (206) 364-5696, fax: (206) 364-5992, www.saferidenews.com

Young Children Magazine, National Association for the Education of Young Children, 1509 16th St. NW, Washington, DC 20036, (202) 232-8777, fax: (202) 328-1846, www.naeyc.org

Consultants and Other Experts

Robert S. Bernstein, Esq., Bernstein Law Firm, PC, #2200 Gulf Tower, Pittsburgh, PA 15219, (412) 456-8100, fax: (412) 456-8135, e-mail: bob@bernsteinlaw.com

Vicki L. Helmick, CPA, 1312 Sterling Oaks Dr., Casselberry, FL 32792, (407) 695-3400, www.accountant-city.com/vicki-helmick-cpa

Doris McNeill, Kids on Wheels Inc., start-up kit with forms and more for a children's transportation service, www.kidsonwheels.net

Credit Card Services

American Express Merchant Services, (888) 829-7302, www.americanexpress.com

Discover Card Merchant Services, (800) 347-6673, www.discovercard.com

MasterCard, (914) 249-4843, www.mastercard.com

PayPal, www.paypal.com

Visa, (800) VISA-311, ext. 96, www.visa.com

Equipment and Supplies

Childcraft Education Corp., furniture, infant/toddler equipment, play equipment, arts and crafts supplies, games, books, and educational materials, P.O. Box 3239, Lancaster, PA 17604, (800) 631-5652, fax: (888) 532-4453, www.childcraft education.com

Kaplan Early Learning Co., classroom and playground equipment, and educational resources, 1310 Lewisville-Clemmons Rd., Lewisville, NC 27023, (800) 334-2014, www.kaplanco.com

Lakeshore Learning Materials, furniture, play equipment, games, and educational items for infants, toddlers, and school-age children, 2695 E. Dominguez St., Carson, CA 90895, (800) 421-5354, fax: (310) 537-5403, www.lakeshorelearning.com. *Note*: In addition to online and print catalogs, Lakeshore has retail outlets across the country.

School Specialty, administrative supplies, arts and crafts materials, furniture, indoor and playground equipment, teacher's aids, and curriculum materials, W6316 Design Dr., Greenville, WI 54942, (888) 388-3224, fax: (888) 388-6344, www.schoolspecialty.com

Government Agencies and Related Resources

Child Care Bureau, U.S. Department of Health & Human Services, Administration for Children & Families, 370 L'Enfant Plaza SW, Washington, DC 20447, www.acf.hhs.gov/programs/ccb

Code of Federal Regulations, www.gpoaccess.com

Environmental Protection Agency, 401 M St. SW, Washington, DC 20460, www .epa.gov. *Note*: Contact for a list of restricted chemicals that are unsuitable for use in a child-care environment and for programs to teach youngsters about the environment.

National Transportation Safety Board, 490 L'Enfant Plaza SW, Washington, DC 20594, (202) 314-6000, www.ntsb.gov

U.S. Consumer Product Safety Commission (CPSC), Washington, DC 20207, (800) 638-2772, www.cpsc.gov. *Note*: Sign up online to receive notification of CPSC recalls.

U.S. Department of Agriculture, Child and Adult Care Food Program, 3101 Park Center Dr., Room 819, Alexandria, VA 22302, (703) 305-2286, www.usda.gov

U.S. Government Printing Office, Superintendent of Documents, Washington, DC 20402, www.gpo.gov

U.S. Patent and Trademark Office, Washington, DC 20231, (800) 786-9199, (703) 308-4357, www.uspto.gov

Successful Child-Care and Transportation Service Providers

Children's Discovery Center and Discovery Express: Where Children Learn Through Exploration, Lois Mitten Rosenberry, 3905 Talmadge Rd., Toledo, OH 43606, www.childrensdiscoverycenters.com

Christine's Day Care, Christine Srabian, Maryland

Gingerbread House, Janet Hale, 137 N. Orange, Exeter, CA 93221, (559) 594-5566

Kids on Wheels Inc., Doris McNeill, 3330 N.W. 30 Pl., Gainesville, FL 32605, www.kidsonwheels.net

Suzanne Wright, Ellicott City, Maryland

Glossary

Add-on child restraint system: any portable child restraint system.

Aseptic technique: the use of procedures that prevent contamination of an object, fluid, or person with infectious microorganisms.

Asphyxial crib death: death attributed to an item within the crib that caused deprivation of oxygen or obstruction to normal breathing of an infant.

Asphyxiation: death or unconsciousness due to inadequate oxygenation, the presence of noxious agents, or other obstructions to normal breathing.

Assessment: an in-depth appraisal conducted to diagnose a condition or determine the importance or value of a procedure.

Asymptomatic: without symptoms.

Backless child restraint system: a child restraint, other than a belt-positioning seat, that consists of a seating platform that does not extend up to provide a cushion for the child's back or head and has a structural element designed to restrain forward motion of the child's torso in a forward-impact crash.

▲

Bacteria: organisms that can survive in and out of the body; they are much larger than viruses and can usually be treated effectively with antibiotics (plural of bacterium).

Bacteriostatic: having the ability to inhibit the growth of bacteria.

Bleach solution for disinfecting environmental surfaces: one-quarter cup of household liquid chlorine bleach (sodium hypochloride) in one gallon of water, prepared fresh daily.

Body fluids: urine, feces, saliva, blood, nasal discharge, eye discharge, and injury or tissue discharge.

Bronchitis: an inflammation or swelling of the tubes leading into the lungs, often caused by a bacterial or viral infection.

Built-in child restraint system: a child restraint system that is designed to be an integral part of and permanently installed in a motor vehicle.

Cardiopulmonary resuscitation (CPR): emergency measures, including closed-chest cardiac compressions and mouth-to-mouth ventilation in a regular sequence, performed by a person on another person whose breathing or heart activity has stopped.

Caregiver: the primary staff who work directly with the children; that is, director, teacher, aide, or others in the center and the child-care provider in small and large family child-care homes.

Carrier: a person who carries within the body a specific disease-causing organism, who has no symptoms of disease, and who can spread the disease to others.

Center: a facility that provides care and education for any number of children in a non-residential setting and is open on a regular basis (i.e., not a drop-in facility).

Child-care resource and referral agencies (R&Rs): local agencies designed to provide support, assistance, and referral information to family child-care providers and centers.

Child restraint system: any device except regular seat belts designed for use in a motor vehicle or aircraft to restrain, seat, or position children who weigh 50 pounds or less.

Child-to-staff ratio: the maximum number of children permitted per caregiver.

Children with special needs: children with developmental disabilities, mental retardation, emotional disturbance, sensory or motor impairment, or significant chronic illness who require special health surveillance or specialized programs, interventions, technologies, or facilities.

Claims-made policy: an insurance policy that provides coverage for liability if the incident occurred and the claim for damages is first made during the policy period; see occurrence policy.

Cohorting toys: keeping toys used by a group of children together for use only by that group of children.

Communicable disease: a disease caused by a microorganism (bacterium, virus, fungus, or parasite) that can be transmitted from person to person via an infected body fluid or respiratory spray, with or without an intermediary agent (e.g., louse, mosquito) or environmental object (e.g., table surface).

Communicable period: the period of time when an infected person is capable of spreading infection to another person.

Compliance: the act of carrying out a recommendation, policy, or procedure.

Congenital: existing from the time of birth.

Conjunctivitis (pinkeye): inflammation (redness and swelling) of the delicate tissue that covers the inside of the eyelids and the eyeball.

Contamination: the presence of infectious microorganisms in or on the body, on environmental surfaces, on articles of clothing, or in food or water.

Contraindication: something (as a symptom or condition) that makes a particular treatment or procedure inadvisable.

Corporal punishment: pain or suffering inflicted on the body (e.g., spanking).

Croup: spasms of the airway that cause difficult breathing and a cough sounding like a seal's bark.

Decibel: the unit of measure of the volume of sounds.

Declarations: the section of an insurance policy that provides basic descriptive information about the insured person or property, the premium to be paid, the time period of the coverage, and the policy limits.

Deductible: a provision in an insurance contract stating that the insurer will pay the amount of any insured loss that exceeds a specific amount; that specified amount is the deductible.

Dermatitis: an inflammation of the skin due to irritation or infection.

Diarrhea: an increased number of abnormally loose stools in comparison with the individual's usual bowel habits.

Disinfect: to eliminate virtually all germs from inanimate surfaces through the use of chemicals (e.g., products registered with the U.S. Environmental Protection Agency as "disinfectants") or physical agents (e.g., heat). In the child-care environment, a solution of one-quarter cup of household liquid chlorine bleach added to one gallon of tap water and prepared fresh daily is an effective disinfectant for environmental surfaces and other inanimate objects that have been contaminated with body fluids, provided that the surfaces have first been cleaned of organic material before disinfecting.

Drop-in care: sporadic care for less than 10 hours per week and no more than once a week.

Ectoparasite: an organism that lives on the outer surface of the body.

Emergency response practices: procedures used to call for emergency medical assistance, to reach parents or emergency contacts, to arrange for transfer to medical assistance, and to render first aid to an injured person.

Endorsement: relative to insurance, an amendment or addition to the policy, also known as a rider.

Evaluation: impressions and recommendations formed after a careful appraisal and study.

Exclusion: denying admission of an ill child or staff member to a facility; relative to insurance, a clause that narrows the focus and eliminates specific coverages that are broadly stated in the policy.

Excretion: waste material that is formed and eliminated from the body, such as feces and urine.

Facility: a legal definition meaning the buildings, funds, equipment, and people involved in providing child care.

Failure-to-thrive syndrome: failure of a child to develop mentally and physically.

Family child care: a homebased child-care business.

Fecal-oral transmission: transmission of a germ from an infected person's stool (bowel movement) into another person's mouth to infect him or her; this transmission usually occurs when the infected person fails to wash his or her hands after having a bowel movement and then handles things (e.g., food or toys) that other people subsequently put in their mouths.

Fever: an elevation of body temperature.

Fine motor activity: small physical motions, such as writing, manipulating small toys, and conducting personal grooming activities; see gross motor activity.

Food-borne pathogen: a germ contained in a food product that is transmitted to persons eating the food.

Fungi: plantlike organisms, such as yeasts, molds, mildews, and mushrooms that get their nutrition from other living organisms or from dead organic matter.

Gross motor activity: large physical motions, such as running, climbing, jumping, and other forms of play; see fine motor activity.

Ground fault circuit interrupter: a piece of equipment in an electrical line that offers protection against electrocution if the line comes into contact with water.

Group size: the number of children assigned to a caregiver or team of caregivers occupying an individual classroom or well-defined space within a larger room.

Health-care provider: a health professional licensed to write prescriptions (e.g., a physician, nurse practitioner, or physician's assistant).

Health consultant: a physician, certified pediatric or family nurse practitioner, or registered nurse who has pediatric or child-care experience and is knowledgeable in child care, licensing, and community resources; provides guidance and assistance to child-care staff on health aspects of the facility.

Health plan: a written document that describes emergency health and safety procedures, general health policies and procedures, and policies covering the management of mild illness, injury prevention, and occupational health and safety.

Hygiene: protective measures taken by individuals to promote health and limit the spread of infectious diseases.

Immunizations: vaccines that are given to children and adults to help them develop protection (antibodies) against specific infections.

Impervious: an adjective describing a smooth surface that does not become wet or retain soil.

Incubation period: the time between exposure to an infectious microorganism and the beginning of symptoms.

Infant: a child between the time of birth and the age of ambulation, usually zero to 12 months old.

Infection: a condition caused by the multiplication of an infectious agent in the body.

Infectious: anything capable of causing an infection.

Infested: having parasites (such as lice or scabies) living on the outside of the body.

Influenza ("flu"): an acute viral infection of the respiratory tract.

Injury, intentional: physical damage to a human being resulting from an intentional event (one done deliberately) including a transfer of energy (physical, chemical, or heat energy).

▲

Injury, unintentional: physical damage to a human being resulting from an unintentional event (one not done deliberately) involving a transfer of energy (physical, chemical, or heat energy).

Isolation: the physical separation of an ill person from other persons to prevent or lessen contact between other persons and the isolated person's body fluids.

Jaundice: yellowing of the eyes or skin.

Large, family child-care home: usually, care and education for 7 to 12 children (including preschool children of the caregiver) in the home of the caregiver who employs one or more qualified adult assistants to meet the child-to-staff ratio requirements; this type of care is likely to resemble center care in its organization of activities.

Lethargy: unusual sleepiness or listlessness in a child.

Liability: legal responsibility for damage or injury; the responsibility is usually financial and usually due to negligence.

Liability limits: the maximum dollar amount an insurance company will pay for claims on a particular policy.

Lice: parasites that live on the surface of the human body (in head, body, or pubic hair).

Occurrence policy: an insurance policy that provides coverage for liability that occurs during the policy period, no matter when the claim is made, even if the policy has expired or the child-care provider has gone out of business; see claims-made policy.

Parasite: an organism that lives on or in another living organism (e.g., ticks, lice, and mites).

Pediatric first aid: emergency care and treatment of an injured child before definite medical and surgical management can be secured.

Pediculosis: louse infestation.

Potable: suitable for drinking.

Preschooler: a child between the age of toilet training and the age of entry into a regular school, usually 36 to 59 months old.

R&Rs: an abbreviation for child-care resource and referral agencies.

Rescue breathing: the process of breathing air into the lungs of a person who has stopped breathing; this process is also called artificial respiration.

Sanitize: to remove filth or soil and small amounts of certain bacteria. For an inanimate surface to be considered sanitary, the surface must be clean, and the number of germs must be reduced to such a level that disease transmission by that surface is unlikely. This procedure is less rigorous than disinfection and is applicable to a wide variety of routine housekeeping procedures involving, for example, bedding, bathrooms, kitchen countertops, floors, and walls. Soap, detergent or abrasive cleaners may be used to sanitize. A number of EPA-registered "detergent sanitizer" products are also appropriate for sanitizing. Directions on product labels should be followed closely.

School-age child: a child who is enrolled in a regular school, including kindergarten, usually 5 to 12 years old.

School-age child-care facility: a center offering a program of activities before and after school and/or during vacations.

SIDS: see Sudden Infant Death Syndrome.

Small, family child-care home: usually, the care and education of one to six children (including preschool children of the caregiver) in the home of the caregiver where programs are modeled either on a nursery school or on a skilled parenting model.

Small, family child-care home network: a group of small family child-care homes in one management system.

Special facility for ill children: a facility that cares only for ill children or a facility that cares for more than six ill children at a time; this is not the same as child care for ill children provided by the child's regular center, large, family child-care home, or small, family child-care home.

Stacked cribs: cribs that are assembled like bunk beds and can be stacked three or four cribs high; not recommended for hygiene reasons.

Standing orders: orders written in advance by a health-care provider that describe the procedure to be followed in defined circumstances.

Substitute staff: caregivers (often without prior training or experience) hired for one day or for an extended period of time who work under direct supervision of a trained permanent caregiver.

Sudden Infant Death Syndrome (SIDS): the sudden and unexpected death of an apparently healthy infant, typically occurring between the ages of 3 weeks and 5 months and not explained by an autopsy.

Syrup of ipecac: a type of medicine that induces vomiting in a person who has swallowed a toxic or poisonous substance.

Systemic: pertaining to a whole body rather than to one of its parts.

Toddler: a child between the age of ambulation and the age of toilet training, usually 13 to 35 months old.

Underimmunized: a person who has not received the appropriate number or types of immunizations for his or her age.

▲

Universal precautions: a term that describes the infectious control precautions recommended by the Centers for Disease Control to be used in all situations to prevent transmission of blood-borne germs (e.g., human immunodeficiency virus and hepatitis B virus).

Vacuum breaker: a device put on a pipe containing liquid (e.g., drinking water) to prevent the liquid from being sucked backward within the pipe.

Virus: a microscopic organism, smaller than a bacterium, that may cause disease; viruses can grow or reproduce only in living cells.

Volunteer: in general, a volunteer is a regular member of the staff who is not paid and is not counted in the child-to-staff ratio.

WIC: abbreviation for the U.S. Department of Agriculture's Special Supplemental Food Program for Women, Infants and Children, which provides food supplements and nutrition education to pregnant and breastfeeding women, infants, and young children who are considered to be at nutritional risk due to their level of income and evidence of inadequate diet.

Index